Coming
To Me

art Three – Finding My Self

a brand new world, a Woman who has newly
covered her potential travels the globe in search of
o she truly is. While finding love, wisdom and
ssion, she must choose to honour the woman she has
nd, or risk losing herself once more forever

BY DEBORAH J KELLY

Coming Home

To Me

A Journey of Getting Lost and Coming Home to Me

Part III – Finding My Self

Based on true events of a young Woman's journey of losing and finding herself; overcoming life's challenges on her quest for meaning and purpose

Deborah J. Kelly

ISBN -13: 9798812422295

Published by Deborah J. Kelly

Cover Design by Deborah J. Kelly

Formatting and Layout by Maryam Nawaz

www.deborahjkelly.com

DEDICATION

For my inspiring and beautiful Mother

Even in the darkest of times, your love shone brightly enough for me to find my way out. Your patience, acceptance, understanding, generosity, never-ending encouragement, and support always lay waiting for me, to find in myself what only you could see.

For that, I am eternally grateful XX

In Loving Memory – For our Dearest 'Esther'

This book is dedicated in loving Memory to our dearest family friend, Esther aka 'Her Ladys**t'. There is so much to thank you for. Where ripples of love flow out and live on, long past our earthly existence, the kindness and generosity of it can be felt at home, in our hearts, and far into the distance.

Love, Debbie XXX

CONTENTS

PREFACE

In the mid 2000's my dad died suddenly; a year later I ended an engagement; and a few months after that I went in search of meaning and found my self along the way! In that time, I was given sign after sign that the Universe wanted me to write a book. I would meet random strangers while backpacking and they would later say to me 'Wow, you should write a book', or 'There's a book in you', or 'If you had a book, I would love to read it!'. There are only so many times you can keep hearing it before you must start paying it some attention.

After I arrived home from traveling the world Solo, having found what I was looking for; I went to an incredible Astrologer, here in Dublin. She was able to tell me events in my chart which had already come to pass, and she spoke about events which I could expect to find opportunity in. She then asked me when was I going to write my book? 'How the heck do you even know about that!', I thought? She said it as though we had conversations about it before, as though it was already done or in progress. I explained that I had many signs telling me to write a book, but I had no idea what about. I had some ideas, but none which I felt comfortable with. It was around this time I was already planning another trip away, to the Camino. My Mum offered me to go to a Hay House Writers Workshop in Dublin the same weekend I was planning to go on the Camino, so I declined. The tickets were expensive and not something I would have bought for myself; I hadn't yet accepted I was a writer, and it was all still a little bit of fantasy. The idea of being able to write a whole book seemed like a mountain I wasn't sure I wanted to climb. But once again, the Universe was not giving up on me, and even my Mum could see there was something written in the stars. On a weekend away I injured my feet, and this meant my Camino trip was no more. My Mam decided to buy the tickets for Hay House, so we went along.

That weekend was the most intensely bizarre experience! I was watching the Universe act in real time! The opening video came on, as we all settled ourselves in our seats, and the video said: 'There is no better time to write a book, than now!'. I felt overwhelmed with emotion and cried silently to myself. It was strange, as though it took me by surprise. Something really struck a chord with me! A writer called Robert Holden, was a guest speaker at the workshop. He got up on stage and asked us all to write a small paragraph starting with 'I write because....'. He gave us 5 minutes and then picked one person randomly, from each seating section, to read their piece. He chose me. I read out loud, shaking at the idea of my inner world being spoken aloud, everyone hearing my depths and words. I had always journaled, written poems and small pieces but never shared it publicly. The microphone shook in my hands as I spoke my words. When I ended, the room erupted in clapping. 'Wow' I thought. I reddened. Robert said, 'I had a story to share' and 'I owed it to my ancestors to share it'! 'What the heck did that mean?' I wondered. But it stayed with me. After Robert, a local Irish celebrity called Bressie, came on stage. He was also as a guest speaker. He was doing a talk about mental health, the darkness we suffer silently, and I cried again. Everything he said resonated so strongly with me. The darkness, the not fitting in, the sadness and lack of confidence. The unspoken words that each of us needed to let out to be free. I cried and knew there was something more happening within me. There was a shift.

That whole weekend I kept meeting random strangers who purposely came over to speak with me. One woman came to me, outside the bathroom, to tell me she loved what I had written and how I spoke. Another woman came over to me and my Mum to say she would love to read my book – even though I hadn't yet written anything! Another woman came over to me while I was grabbing a water and said, 'Oh! It's you! I wanted to talk to you and tell you that your words touched my heart! I can't wait to read your book!' I was floored. It was nuts! If ever I needed a sign that I was meant to write a book, it seemed this was it. At the very end of the weekend, just as we were waiting for the crowds to leave, a woman came up to me and gave me her business card. She was the commissioning editor of Hay House UK and said if I didn't have time to write for their competition, I should contact her as soon as I had my book started or done. I was blown away! I knew there and then I needed to write a book.

Over the course of the following year, I did everything I could to avoid writing the book. I visited the Astrologer again, and once more she said, 'Is the book finished?'. My stars were showing opportunities for communications and publications. I have, over the years, been told time and time again from Shamans, Mystics and Psychics and alternative Healers that I have an incredible light and energy within; that I would not be able to hide in the shadows anymore and I had a role to play. I was to be seen publicly, and I wouldn't like it because I preferred the side-lines. I was told many times I would be successful and not to fear following my path; that my Ancestors were waiting for me to speak the truth they never could. This all began to make sense to me. I was petrified and it felt horribly uncomfortable, but I had been in search of meaning and wasn't likely to shut the door in its face, if this was it.

In honesty I avoided writing this book. In fact, I tried to come up with lots of other ideas on what I could write about. Deep down, however, I knew this was the one, it had to come out. In a way, I needed to write it to clear the decks for what's to come: for the books that need to be written after this. Since finishing this book, the next book has already begun. The labour pains are threatening it to be written. It's like a wild animal, coming closer and closer. I have the idea, yet I can't see it clearly, but we are getting comfortable with each other. It's letting me know it's there to be written. Funnily enough, it won't give itself to me until this one is finished. As soon as this book was nearly finished, I could see myself running away, distracting myself with other things. I could see how I was avoiding finishing it off at all costs because that would mean I had to decide whether I would publish it or not. What made me not want to publish? With every sharing of the truth is the risk of fallout and destruction of many relationships. However, I have had to carefully weigh up the pros and cons. I always swore to myself, if I could ever find a way out of the pain I experienced, I would share it with other women. This is my book, for them.

My truth caused a lot of pain many years ago and pushing it to one side allowed everyone to move on. I am aware I am opening it all up again. Here I am standing in front of everyone, taking the risk of once again being rejected for speaking my truth. As a kid I didn't have that choice and I silenced myself. As an adult who now knows and understands the role of the abused; they are always the one who suffer in silence. We choose to come to this earth and have a set of experiences; the people we meet along the way are part of that journey. I blame nobody for what happened in my past; I believe that we have soul contracts we come into this world to fill and there is a lesson in everything. I believe and feel I have done justice in conveying my perspective and understanding for everyone's situation; it is the only way to be fair for all involved. I just ask those who feel conflicted in reading this book: be objective. When not emotionally attached to the story it is possible to feel compassion for the protagonist; however, when there is attachment there is fear, and fear of blame, guilt, and feelings of misunderstanding. This book is a means of me writing my truth and allowing my story to help others who have felt unheard, who are looking to find themselves; to help those who are lost, find hope in a way back home to themselves. These books are intended as a tool for healing - therefore: - if you want your world to stay the same and not look at any other perspective, then you should not read this book. However, if you choose to be open to the concept of there being several perspectives and views, and a new way of experiencing life, of understanding we all have our own journey, then please go ahead, and read this book, and/or all 3 books.

To media, or anybody who wishes to discuss the book, I will advise, in advance, this book is meant to resonate with those who feel they have lost themselves on their journey through life. It is meant as a means of showing how lost you can truly be in yourself, yet the soul always wants you feel peace; it always wants you to find your way home. Even the darkest emotions are guideposts back home. The heaviest of emotions are there to make you ask yourself questions, tough questions, and to keep exploring and discovering so you can find your way back. I had to surrender and lose myself completely before I was ready to find myself. When I did, it was as though a door opened. Life is a journey and I admit I don't have all the answers. I am still discovering and exploring; as long as I breathe, I will continue to do so. I will get it wrong, and I will get it right. I will fall off the wagon and lose contact with my inner guidance, and I will come back to it. But now that I know what it feels like to find it, I can never be truly lost: just temporarily misplaced.

To those reading this book, who are thinking of writing their own stories and would like to write their own book... DO IT! It has been the single most therapeutic and empowering thing I have ever done. In truth, the book wrote me. What I discovered as I began to write (not knowing the true direction it was taking) was that my body shook, and shivered, trembled, became cold and agitated as I wrote certain parts. I saw myself intentionally avoid sitting to write. I saw myself get up and down 20 times before writing certain parts. I procrastinated for weeks on some parts. In the end, it was only the starting which was the most difficult. When I was in the flow of writing, it was like therapy. The thoughts were worse than the reality of writing itself.

I grew so much from being present with myself through the process; seeing how my mood changed at just the thoughts of sitting down to write the most difficult parts. My body was once again protecting me. I literally felt as though I went through PTSD while writing some parts of this book. My body released emotions. My mind was clear and focused. I was present and calm. All the while my body reacted in ways I couldn't have ever imagined. While my mind was clear, I saw my own moods shift and change for 'no reason', but of course it was release of emotions and stuck energy.

In the journey through writing this book I felt as though me and my body became better acquainted. I saw how it has so often reacted, in terribly subtle changes, and ways to tell me that I feel uncomfortable; even when my mind feels clear. I have begun the journey of getting to know myself, and it is never too late for anyone to do the same.

Growth is about accepting the light and dark side of life: the light and dark sides of ourselves. It is about seeing that both the light and dark are born from the same place; they are merely signposts and lessons which helps us to grow. Yes, there are tough lessons we go through in life, but there is always something to be learned. The Universe will never give us anything we can't handle. We have all survived every challenge we have ever met, to date.

While on a spiritual path or road of self-development I can say with certainty that I will learn many lessons; I will forget as many, then re-learn them, re-apply them, and continue to grow. There will be some days where we may feel as though all our hard work has been undone. On other days we feel we are fully through the other side of it. Then, something small triggers us and there we are back again with old emotions and triggers. What's important is to be present and patient with ourselves, in the same way we would with a child. Have compassion, love and understanding. These are the most beautiful parts of being human. We are never perfect. We all make mistakes. We all have our own stories, and we all have our darkness as well as our light. It is accepting these parts of ourselves and others; by not being afraid to look at these parts in ourselves and others; by not avoiding and feeling fearful of how these things may change us or others; and holding space, that allows us growth.

I asked a friend of mine, Erica, recently if she had one word for me what would it be? 'You're an Explorer Debs!' she said with such beautiful wonderment and enthusiasm! So, I endeavour to always forge my way through life like an intrepid explorer of the body, mind, and soul.

I truly hope this book inspires you; shows you how, even though all of life's ups and downs, there are lessons to be learned which make us stronger in everything we do. We are all on our own unique paths and ultimately, we are all just trying to find our way back home. We are trying to find our way back to ourselves and the light within. In doing so it may not be perfect, it may not happen immediately and when we want it, but it will happen when its right. We may temporarily lose ourselves along the way, and that's okay; it's part of the journey. When we learn to reconnect with that little voice within and learn to tap into what feels right and wrong for us in our world; to live through our hearts more than our minds, we learn and understand that what feels right inside. What's right for one, may not be the same for another; we can celebrate our differences with love and respect. If not, then there is a lesson in that by itself and all it is, is another signpost leading you back home through another path.

Finally, I hope if you feel you have received some healing, wisdom, or insight from these books, that you will share them with your friends, loved ones and family. I would also love to know how they have inspired or helped you on your journey. Stay connected with Deborah J. Kelly on Social Media or online & Join her Newsletter on www.deborahjkelly.com. Love and Light, Deborah J. Kelly XXX.

***

Coming Home To Me

A Journey of Getting Lost
and Coming Home to Me

Part III: Finding My Self

CHAPTER ONE

THE MEANING OF LIFE

I lay on the bed in my bedroom, it was dark and lonely and I felt lost in myself. I had no more fight left in me - Tom had taken it all. But I had to keep going. I had no choice. I wanted it all to end but my body kept on living. I wanted to leave this place and craved for the peace and lightness in Spirit, that an end would bring. I had a kind of homesickness in myself, a craving to go back to that place before birth and after death. I wanted it all to end and be free of the weight of this world. This life seemed so thick and heavy with emotions. I had reached a point where I didn't understand the whole meaning or purpose of this life.

The longing to go home seemed to grow. It seemed to be more constant and intense. I felt useless in life and felt useless in relationships, I never seemed to get it right. It always felt that people would tire of me the more they knew of me. It was as though the more time spent together with me, the less appealing I was to them. And there it was again, that feeling of loathing and hatred for myself. That seeing of myself, as easily disposal and pointless. My rejection of my own self. That self-loathing and hatred for my existence. I wanted so much to be loved by somebody, adored by them the way I adored them. All I wanted was to be enough. To be enough, so they didn't want anybody else. To be enough for them, so I could feel I was enough. To feel enough for myself. I hated that I couldn't get it right. I hated these feelings and I hated that no matter what happened, eventually people just didn't like me, and became bored of me. The feelings of wanting to escape myself was banging loudly on the doors inside my mind, asking to be let in. It was a battle. It only ever seemed a matter of time before I was out in the cold again. It had seemed that Tom had done the same in many respects. I questioned everything. Did he not fancy me? Had I gone too fat? Did he not like me? Was it my eczema? Was it the sex issues? Was I not who he wanted…? Was I too much, too intense, too sensitive, too defensive? Who did he want? What did they have that I didn't? Was I not enough…? Why was I not enough!?

I can feel the tears welling up and sticking in my throat as I write this. Somehow, I feel I have always struggled with the panic and fear that I won't be enough or wanted by others, that I will get in deep and then I'll be discarded. It was an old wound, and the darkness liked to help me hate on myself by reminiscing on those feelings.

In the darkness of my room and my mind, the more I felt it the less I could fight it off. It had grown stronger than my will to stay here. I was running out of reasons to stay, and it seemed to overshadow any reasoning I had with myself. I even began to research the most pain free ways to go. I just had no interest in hanging around. I even began to reason that my Mum would be okay; I was sure she would understand the pain I was in and why I wanted to leave. I was sure she would have known I was happier where I had gone, and I certainly thought I would have been! She has always known me to a be a deep little thing, a sensitive soul, and has seen my struggles with this world so I was sure she would forgive me. I also knew that was a dangerous place to go in my mind. To reach the point that I was ready to leave, I was conscious and aware and present in myself. I had thought about it with a clear mind, and that's a point I had not reached before that moment.

I find this place such a difficult place to be at times. The pace at which we, as humans, are steamrolling to our own destruction is phenomenal and it makes me sad. People are so unnecessarily cruel at times to each other, we are losing ourselves to technology, money and greed, and the softness to life has been swapped for hard corners of stress, anger, sadness, grief and frustration. I thought of how I was working to live and living to work. This crazy-ass world of 9-5 made no sense at all. To work crazy hours, with crazy customers, with little or no down time, only for it to make me crazy! It made no sense at all. I thought of how myself and Tom were living in the train tracks of life, aiming to do what everyone else was doing - job, car, marriage, kids, house. But now those tracks were all broken. I was relieved to not have had kids with him, it would have been a disaster.

I had always wanted kids and we were to get cracking at it as soon as we were married. But now, I was grateful to not have had kids in the middle of all of this. It would have been unfair, cruel and unkind. I would have been tied to him forever, they would have had a Dad with serious issues and I'm not sure I would have been comfortable with him being around them. Now, I got to walk away. He had to keep all his craziness! I felt it slapped me into reality and wasn't so sure that having kids was a good idea any longer. This world was changing at lightning speed, and to be honest in general even outside of my own mess, I wasn't so sure I liked the world we were heading toward. It seemed dogmatic, unkind, stressed out, emotionally thick, oppressive and if I didn't want to be here most of the time, then why would I want to bring kids into the world? To me, I felt more maternal not having kids. I was keeping them safer and happier, by not bringing them into this world. Something serious would have to change before I could change my mind on this, the world would need to change. I would need to change.

Having nothing more to hold onto, and no struggle left in me. I lay on the bed and asked the Universe to take me. I was giving up. I lay there hoping life would melt away from me, upon request…. You can imagine I was very disappointed when, after a good 5 minutes of offering myself up to the Ether, I was still alive! I lay there realising I was in limbo. I no longer had any emotions, no desires, no attachments, nothing. I felt lifeless but my heart was still beating and my lungs still breathing. I felt as though life was happening to me but I had no interest in participating with it. I reasoned with the Universe that if she really wanted me to stay, she would have to find a reason, or show me some sense of purpose, because I was beyond looking for it anymore. I was no longer searching, just existing.

Then, in that moment, it was though a light turned on inside the darkness of my mind. The word 'Travel' appeared in my mind, like a golden beacon of hope, which came from nowhere. It blinked again in my mind 'Travel', and now it had my attention. I could feel my face soften, become animated with curiosity, and my heart soften with hope for a moment. 'Travel', yes, there it was again! I sat up in the bed now. In the darkness of my bedroom I could feel the warmth of its hope breathe life into my veins, into my solar plexus, into my heart. Although I had been travelling before, I had always intended and wanted to go travelling alone, something which I felt was no longer an option when getting married and starting a family. It struck me that now would be an ideal time. I was free and single, I had no house ties, no kids, and I had money from the wedding, which I had saved up. It made sense that if I was now the most alone, I could ever have been in the world, that perhaps I could take back control of that loneliness and chose to be alone travelling instead. Yes! That was it!

I had hope!

The coming weeks were spent with a new sense of life and enthusiasm. I even had a thirst and lust for life. I had dreams to fill and memories to be made. New memories. I would get to know me, all by myself. I would be alone and make decisions alone, with no influence or encouragement from others. I would be free of the expectations, oppressions, opinions and emotions of others. There was nobody to let me down, nobody to be, other than myself, for me. I was curious to see how I would navigate my life, how I would move in the world. I was excited to become an observer of my own self; without the influence of others. I was curious to see, whether alone, I would be more into museums, cities, jungles, trekking, lazing on a beach etc. I wondered, without the influence of others, where would I go and what would I do! Being completely alone, it thrilled me suddenly! I felt a passion for life that I had not ever felt before, it was a passion to live! Travel literally saved my life.

***

CHAPTER TWO

LET THE TRAVELS COMMENCE

began to look up all the various countries I could travel to. What I could see and do in each country. I felt like a kid in a candy shop and didn't know where to start. A guy in work, who was into alternative thinking, self-development, philosophy and all things mind, body, soul, had been talking out loud in the office about Ayahuasca. I had never heard of it before, but it sounded as though it was a big red reset button for the soul... it was just what I needed! I had tried so many therapies over the years and none seemed to work, none seemed to 'fix' me, maybe this would give me some peace and help me reset from all that had just happened. So, I began to look into it more seriously.

Ayahuasca is a plant medicine brew, made with the Ayahuasca vine, also known as 'Vine of the soul', and also typically made with Chacruna leaves. It is used by the Shamans of the Amazon, in South America for ceremonial purposes, in order to gain greater connection with Pachamama and Spirit. It is a plant medicine for which people can gain enlightenment, release, and purge aspects of their lives in which they feel stuck. The brew is made ceremonially, whilst the Shamans are on a Dieta (Shamanic Diet). It contains Dimethyltryptamine, also known as DMT or the Spirit Molecule, (which is a chemical found in all living plants and animals in varying amounts) and MAOI, Monoamine oxidase inhibitor, which stops the breakdown of DMT, allowing it to reach the brain. When MAOI is combined with DMT, it allows the benefits of the DMT to stay longer in the body, thus allowing the experience more time, space, clarity and awareness. In essence Ayahuasca brew has an Entheogenic effect, which means it induces alterations in perception, mood, consciousness, cognition, or behaviour for the purposes of engendering spiritual development. It was used to gain insight into our purpose, into blockages that may be stopping us from living our true potential, and a purge of even the most stubborn of knots. Shamans in the Amazon used this as a ceremonial healing modality to help those in their community who were ill, mentally, psychically and spiritually. They used it to search for answers and for general healing.

There were many Ayahuasca centres all over Peru and having done a lot of research I decided to go for a less commercial, more authentic retreat in Iquitos. It was on a little island called Padre Cocha, to a retreat centre called 'Selva Madre'. I knew I had to start my trip with Ayahuasca. It was a master plant and would have some profound teachings for me, so I felt it was better to start with this on my journey to see what would lie ahead as a result of my working with Mother Aya.

As I was researching and planning, My Uncle Mick, or Hobo as I call him, from Melbourne, Australia got in touch with me and offered me to go into the Aussie Outback, on a one-month camping trip. He had no idea of his timing, it was serendipitous, and of course I had to say Yes! Hobo was actually a 4th cousin once removed, on my Dad's side. He was a bachelor in his 70s and had backpacked most of the US, Canada, Alaska, Africa, crossing the Sahara Dessert on foot, and Europe through his younger years. His military short red hair had now mostly faded into strands of golden white, like the faded sand dunes of time. The well weathered lines on his tanned face told stories of his outdoor adventures, and although Hobo was a pretty crass and brash bachelor his whole life, he was a marshmallow inside which very few saw. He had a real soft spot for me, and I just loved him to bits. He was hard work, very set in his ways, and I knew the trip would be tough, but well worth it. He had messaged to tell me there was a trip himself and my Dad were supposed to make together. His faithful friend 'Bo Diddly Dog', who he travelled most years into the outback with alone, was now gone, and he felt it might be a nice thing for us both to make that trip to the outback together. We would do it in memory of them both. His timing couldn't have been better. So, I told him he was "on" and I planned to be with him in July. My travel plans were coming together.

Now all I needed was to figure out where else I wanted to go, what else I wanted to do and when was the best time to go. After some research I decided that I would start in Peru with Ayahuasca, then fly to Oz to spend a month in the outback with Mick, and from there my plans were loose. I had thought about the option of living and working in Oz. I was sadly over the age for getting a work visa, but there were plans to change the legal visa age in the coming months, which meant I may still be eligible. So, I decided to see what happened. I knew the other countries I wanted to go to, but it would all depend on the work visa in Oz and time of the year I would leave there.

I contacted a few travel companies here in Ireland and none of them seemed to have much experience in the countries I wanted to travel to, or I didn't feel a good rapport with them. I could hear in their voices they were winging it and doing their best to sell me on the areas they knew, rather than the areas I wanted to go. My trip was a little unusual, the route was not the normal backpacker experience, and I was determined to find a way of making the trip work how I wanted it to, not how somebody else wanted it to. I was becoming impatient and frustrated, as by now I just wanted to get the hell out of Ireland. There were too many reasons to move forward, rather than stay stagnant. I needed a change, a new life and a new outlook on life. I wanted to book the trip already, hand in my notice to work and move on to the next phase of my life. I knew better times were around the corner, and by now I was itching to get going. The sense of freedom I felt at simply planning the trip was liberating. However, I still had obstacles in that my health had deteriorated somewhat over the past number of months. The worse the symptoms got the more nervous I became, I wondered at times how I would even read the flight boards in an airport, that's how bad my eyes were. But somehow, I knew I just needed to push past it all, the idea of travel had given me a new lease of life I couldn't go back to the darkness of my life to that point.

I had been for medical tests, lots and lots of tests, and they all came back with nothing terribly exciting to report. Because there seemed to be no rhyme or reason to my physical symptoms, I was sent for an MRI. It appeared that I had a 12mm Pineal Cyst on the Pineal gland in my brain, which is only about 4-5m size in itself. So, the growth was quite significant. However, apparently 'Penelope the Pineal Cyst', as I called her, had nothing to do with my sight, memory or ill health. In fact, apparently it would have no effect on me. This was very frustrating as I had dug more and more, and yet there was no answers to what was going on. It concerned me my health was going to mess with my ability to travel alone, but my will to live and see the world, decided to ignore it all and go anyway. So, I continued in search of a travel agent who could help me plan the trip I wanted, not the trip they wanted to plan for me!

I decided as I was doing a round-the-world trip, I wasn't limited to simply buying those tickets in Ireland. Surely any company worldwide, who look after worldwide travel, could book those tickets, and who knows I may have even been able to get them a little cheaper elsewhere too. So, I contacted a company in the US, a company in Spain and a company in the UK. After a few days I got an email from a guy called Piers in Travel

Station, a company based in Brighton, in the UK. He wasn't too pushy or too salesman-ish (I hate feeling like I am being 'SOLD' to) so I gave him a try. He called me that evening around 6pm and we had a chat. He told me he was impressed with my 'Ehhh…. VERY detailed email!'. He said to me: 'You certainly sound like you know what you want, most customers haven't got a clue. I like that'. I had mentioned in the email that I was going to a 'Retreat' in Peru, and it seemed he knew exactly what I was talking about. 'There's only particular kinds of people who go on those retreats, so you sound like a very interesting person', he said with a curiosity in his voice.

I can't deny, that although I had literally just broken up with Tom, I felt a real flutter in my belly for Piers' voice. He had a kind and gentle voice, an English accent which was more south country mixed with London, a country come city boy perhaps? But I was actually quite attracted to it! Thank God he's in the UK, I thought! A flirt would be harmless, especially as I was newly single and with my new lease on life, I felt excited to chat with him.

Piers was very chatty and incredibly helpful; he had been all over the world and I could tell he had been on many adventures.

He too had been to a retreat in Peru and so I guess that's why we clicked. He stayed chatting with me well after office closing time, which impressed me also, and I felt a real connection over the phone. I could hear a voice inside warn me, 'You're in trouble Debs!!!', but I chose to ignore it. He lived in the UK, I reminded myself, AND, I was going travelling anyway.

I had vowed to myself NOT to get into a relationship straight away, as I have a tendency to do that without my intention. Nope, this time I was going to stay single. I was going to get to know myself more, without distractions, and I would date me, myself, for a year…. at the very least! The last time I went away travelling I was in a relationship. I was going out with my mate's brother Darragh for years, and he let me off to gallivant around the world. I was always the monogamous type and so cheating was never on the cards or even a possibility. I would feel guilty over a flirt let alone go further. So, this time I was single and ready to mingle. I had no ties back home and I was alone. I was going to live life without restrictions. That's what I wanted and needed after all that had happened. I deserved to feel free in myself. So, any notion I had over fancying this boy, especially as it was only his voice, was ridiculous!

As it happened, I booked my tickets a month later with Piers. He was so good at his job and I felt safe and secure, that no matter where I was in the world, if I needed him in a jam, he would be on hand. As a solo traveller it was nice to know I had a travel agent who could solve any potential travel issues I might encounter.

***

CHAPTER THREE

AYAHUASCA DREAMING

The months had rolled by and soon I was waving goodbye to my old job, and waving goodbye to my Mum at the airport. I was heading off to Peru. Mam knew I was going to a plant medicine retreat in the Amazon to do something called Ayahuasca, and was very supportive of my choice.

I was impressed that she was so open to me having this experience, considering my Dad's involvement with Anti-Drugs Talks. He used to visit local Primary Schools as a Policeman, when we were kids, and talk to them about the effects of drug use. Both my parents were anti-drugs. Even though Ayahuasca is a plant medicine, it is essentially DMT, and a mind-altering medicine. So I was surprised how cool she was with it all. She seemed to trust me as she knew I was doing it for spiritual reasons.

A few days before I left for Peru, I got her to watch a movie with me. Even though she knew a lot about what I was going to do, I wanted her to watch 'DMT The Spirit Molecule'. It was a movie which would explain Ayahuasca a little more, in hopes that she might be able to understand it. Especially if would be talking about it, when I got back. I wanted her to understant the visual element of things. It…. Was…. Hilarious….!! It made a lot of sense, when we watched the movie together, as to why she had been so understanding. It was only when she realised its effects being hallucinogenic, with visuals, and purging by vomit and diarrhoea, that she seemed a little taken aback… it seemed she had a fair idea, had done some research, but perhaps hadn't realised the extent of what it was! She thought I was going to a kind of meditation or yoga retreat, which had herbal medicine. Her reaction was entertaining to watch as she shaped faces that said 'Wow, and Okay' in the same movement. She told me she hadn't realised it was as 'LSD- like' as that, and seemed cautious. However, in the same breath and sentence as her realisation, she reassured me that she trusted I had done my research. She knew by the way I had spoken about it, and was glad for me to go try something new if it would help me.

There are not many daughters who could say 'I'm off to do some tripping in the jungle now Mam, see you later!', and that shows the level of connection and trust that we had. She knew it was a life or death situation for me, she knew I needed to find myself and knew I needed answers, so she was behind me all the way.

My time in the jungle, working with Mother Aya (Ayahuasca) and the Shamans of the Shipibo Tribes there, had given me a platform from which to dive off. The ceremonies were held at night, when the collective consciousness is clearer and less polluted. We held Dieta, a type of Shamanic diet of clean food and living, before the ceremonies and rested the day after, with quiet reflection to take in what we had experienced, seen, felt etc. Each ceremony was experienced differently for me; each held different meaning and had different messages. Each ceremony allowed me to work on various aspects of blockages in my life. Each ceremony my purges varied from puking to pooping, to both - but all were incredibly cathartic. I worked through many past traumas in my life and although I was not yet clear how this experience had or would affect me long term, I knew it had had a profound effect on me, a shift had taken place.

Of course, I was keen to tell my new Travel Agent about my experiences, so we could compare poop and puke stories, yet it was so difficult to put it in to words. I wrote him an email and tried to word it all as best I could.

During the retreat I had had a vision. It was like having a daydream at night time I guess you could call it. I saw Piers in his workplace. He was packing up his things and doing a handover to his colleagues; he was coming out to see me in Malaysia for 3 weeks. I knew it was a bit random, and put it down to random wanderings of my mind. I must have liked him more than I thought. Of course, I decided not to include this in my emails to him! That would be a bit intense and weird, and likely to scare the poor boy away! 'Who's this mad Irish girl having dreams about me when we haven't ever met before', I could almost hear him think.

He sent me back some of his own experiences and before long we were swapping emails to and fro. We decided when I got back to Ireland we would do a Skype chat, as it would be easier than all the emails. I was due to fly on to Australia then, so we could have a chat about the next leg of the trip then too, and what flights I might want him to book for me.

I had 2-3 days back home in Ireland with my Mum before I was jet setting off to the Aussie outback to spend a month or more with Hobo. The night before my flight I did a skype call with Piers. We talked for about 2-3 hours easily; it was as though we had known each other a lifetime. We hadn't noticed the time go by so quickly. As it was getting late we decided we best go our separate ways, as I was up early the next day to fly to Oz. It was a lovely chat and it was nice to see his face. I most definitely fancied him, and having chatted with him so easily, I could feel a childish excitement in my tummy... giddy butterflies! 'What.... The.... Heck?', I thought! I was confused to have these feelings so soon; I was confused because it was incredibly inconvenient and yet I didn't want to ignore them either. So, I decided to send him an email.

It took me 2-3 hours to write and re-write and re-write and re-write it. I was so tired by the end that I decided not to send it. I needed to read it again the next morning, to see how I felt about it with a clear head and good night's sleep. I've always found I do my best, deepest and most authentic thinking at night, but quite often I need to bring those thoughts into the light of day to see what confidence or fears I have around them. I woke the next morning, read it again and decided to press send.

Essentially I had written a very long winded email to tell him I 'kind of fancied him', but expressed it was incredibly inconvenient given my current situation. I told him I felt I needed to get it out there and say it to him, with no expectations of return or something to come of it. I told him I just needed to say it and it was perfectly fine if he didn't feel the same, that it would be business as usual and there was no need for awkwardness. The End.

I caught my flight to Oz, with a stopover in Munich on the way. My bags had gone missing on the connection flight. Where usually I would have flipped out and began to panic, I was calm. I was operating with what I now called 'Ayahuasca Calm'. I had a new found sense of 'it will all be okay, things are unfolding as they are meant to. I knew the calmer I was, the better the outcome'.

Before leaving the Ayahuasca Retreat in Iquitos, Don Lucho our Shaman, had 'Prescribed' everyone their own individual homework to take from our time there, from the ceremonies. For those who had only one ceremony, their prescriptions were for a shorter period of time thereafter. As I had done over 9 ceremonies, I was advised that my 'Prescription' was to be taken for a minimum of 6 -12 months... my prescription was 'Ayahuasca Calm'; to relax and allow anger and impatience to wash over me, come and go. I remember him telling me this, and all I could do was look at him with an open jaw. I repeated the prescription loudly and with emphasis, 'SIX MONTHS!?'. He laughed at me with his big round belly, in a sweet and jovial Peruvian-Santa type of way. He smiled from ear to ear rocking on his chair, then looked at me softly with full confidence and reassured me he had every faith in me.

As I sat waiting now - bagless in Munich - to board my next connection to Melbourne, an email came through. It was from Piers. 'OH! MY! GOD!', I thought! I wanted to both run away and jump up and down, at the same time. I was so excited and so nervous; my stomach was doing cartwheels! I knew as soon as I read that email there was no going back! He said 'Jeez, you really do like to write and go on. I thought you would never get to the point'; my heart sank, I was mortified. I felt so embarrassed. 'It takes a lot of guts to do what you did, and I've been thinking I quite fancy you too!', he continued! Every sense in my body was electric and I thought 'Oh My God!'. I was so excited and so giddy in myself. As I waited in the departure lounge, everyone in their own world, I was secretly high-fiving myself and doing cartwheels of joy! 'He likes me! The boy likes me! Yippee!! OMG! What now... what does that mean?', I thought. So, I emailed him back to say I was relieved to get his email and delighted to hear he liked me. I explained that I had no idea what all this meant, but I was glad we had connected. I reminded him I was traveling and living freedom for the first time in years. He knew I had been engaged before and knew some of the stuff that happened when I was telling him about the Ayahuasca retreat. So, I had nothing to hide and decided if we were honest with each other, then nobody could get hurt.

My plane touched down in Oz and Hobo came to collect me. I was still bagless and so he welcomed me to his home and gave me some of his clothes to wear. I looked like a lumberjack, but it was cold in Oz and I was glad of the extra layers.

I checked my phone the next morning and there was an email in from Piers - again the butterflies came! I had no idea where this was all going; in fact it didn't have anywhere to go, but we decided to just stay in touch and see what happened. He told me he was sorry about the baggage and would do what he could to sort it, but I told him I already had it in hand. He then said 'Look, I know this might seem a little forward but I have some holidays to take from work and had a thought. Seeing you want to go to Malaysia, how about we meet up and go to the Perhenthian Islands for 3weeks? It's somewhere I've always fancied going!'.

'WHAT… THE… ACTUAL… F***!! NO WAY!!', I thought! This was INSANE! My daydream…. my random Ayahuasca daydream…. actually, played out! He was coming to see me in Malaysia, for three weeks! Madness!! So, I rang him to tell him about my crazy dream, and we both knew there was something more to all this.

Over the coming weeks before I headed into the Outback, we were in contact almost every single day. Hobo hated technology, making it very difficult for me to use my phone while I was around him. There was also an 8hr time difference, so it meant that most of our chats were held at 2-3am Ozzie time. This happened under my covers while whispering or messaging back and forth. Alternatively, I would head off on a day trip to the city, to ramble about while enjoying my backpacker's freedom. I brought my laptop with me and would use an internet café so we could chat by video. I remembered chatting with him in a Starbucks in Melbourne city; my heart was pumping and jumping, racing and giddy. I could not stop smiling from ear to ear. My face was almost cramping from the excitement. I would return home to Hobo then, ignoring my phone for any messages or calls, but excited for when one would come through. We were both falling seriously fast and in no time; it honestly felt as though we were in a relationship. I was conscious of the speed and intensity of it all. Having just come out from an apocalyptic engagement. I didn't want Piers to be a rebound - it was more than just that. I knew I needed to cool my boots and come back to reality, so my month's escape to the Outback with Hobo, would give me more time and space.

After 31 days of traveling 8500km of the Ozzie outback with Hobo, we were back to Melbourne. It was an incredible trip. It was also an incredible amount of hard work - but well worth it. Piers and I had, at this stage, remained in touch whenever there was a phone signal, which as you can imagine in the Outback wasn't very often. The hard work and mental pressures of camping every day, with a 70-year-old bachelor who was ex-military and pretty set in his ways, had its challenges. However, I also loved every minute of it, and was so glad to have had that time with Hobo. It was very special and the trip, held in honour of my Dad and The Bo Diddly Dog, meant a lot to us both. In a weird way, as much as we wanted to throttle each other at times, myself and Hobo were also great camping buddies. We had a routine and system to our day, and saw some truly incredible sights, while traversing some seriously intense terrain. The vast open night sky, sleeping under the Milky Way, and watching the stars twinkle was spectacular. All while listening to the crackling of a fire, which we had worked hard to drag wood to and keep going, it was immensly satisfying. Supping a few cold Coopers Sparkling, after making our dinner over the fire and swapping camp stories, is something I would love to do again someday. However, by the end of that trip I wasn't sure whether myself and Hobo would be certifiably sane to go there again. By the end of the month we were both shattered. Among the very many highlights to that trip, which really tested my Ayahuasca calm, was the reward of an odd phone signal every now and then. The signal would boost and sometimes 3-4 messages came in from Piers, which was always such a treat!

He had kept writing messages for me, even when he knew I had no signal. That meants when I got to the next town my phone would beep beep beep, and I'd have lots of messages to read from him, showing me he had been thinking of me. My heart would race and flutter and beat and pump! I absolutely lived for those messages, and whenever we could do a video chat we would sit up until all hours, to get that alone time together. The time difference meant I often caught him before he was going to work and I loved that he wanted to talk to me at any time of the day or night. We had fallen really hard for each other, and we hadn't even met yet! It was as though we had known each other all our lives. We spoke as though we were together as a couple already, and as though we were together for years. Because we did so much communication via text or email, it meant we had to be very clear and verbal about everything. We spoke very openly about our feelings or challenges we faced, and it was refreshing to meet a guy who I could chat so easily, openly, vulnerably and honestly, with.

My trip to the Outback finished and I decided to take a trip to Noosa, a plush little surf town on the east coast of Australia. I had an incredible time with Hobo; it was period of intense growth both physically and emotionally but also mentally. I needed some time out alone, to once again integrate the experiences I had just had. So, I caught a flight to this chilled out surf town for a week of some well-deserved R&R.

While I was in Noosa, I decided to go for some Reflexology. I had never had it done professionally before and found a little centre, not far from the hostel, where they also practiced Cranio-Sacral therapy too. I wanted a nice relaxing spa treatment, but also wanted something a little more functional. I had been studying Acupressure myself for years and loved it! For me, self-healing is such a divine right for us as humans.

We live in an age where we go to the Doctor and take a pill, rather than listen and trust what our bodies are telling us: something I too had to learn. Using traditional therapies and plant medicine, is far more natural for us as human beings; it is more in tune with what our bodies need. Yet because their effects are more subtle and slow - reversing effects in just the same way dis-ease creeps in - we discard them as useless. I had learned a lot about alternative and plant medicine while in Peru. Since working with Ayahuasca, and other plant medicines while there, it seemed I had ignited a new passion and interest in natural healing, which had lay dormant for years.

After my own recent realisations, while working with Ayahuasca, and learning how incredibly intertwined we all are, I began to listen to my own inner guidance. I became incredibly aware of how intelligent the body is; how remarkably intelligent nature is; and how they are always communicating with us if we would only listen: if we only knew how to listen! I had ignored my own body and senses for years, and since going to Peru it was as though a new version of myself was coming forward. It was as though I had begun to discover myself, who I was, and was finally speaking from my soul: from a place that was unjudged and genuine. The real me was coming out without anyone to hide from, or feel nervous about showing myself for who I was. For me, the best way to start was to pay it more attention. So, I decided I would study various therapies in each country I visited. I was a total sucker for alternative therapies and one of my favourite things to do while traveling, was to get a spa or therapy treatment in every country I visited. I loved learning their natural and traditional, local healing modalities. I loved to try out local culture. This was the perfect way to tap into each country's local wisdom. I even took a course, while I was in Melbourne, to study Su-Juk Acupressure, with a crazy Russian man and his wife. They were so lovely, but absolutely nuts!

My Reflexology treatment was AMAZING! I was absolutely floored by how good it was. I got on so well with the Therapist, Peytrah, too. We chatted about all things holistic and alternative. She mentioned she had a friend who did Meditation on the beach at sunrise every morning. She offered me to join them. I agreed, and the next morning I went down to the beach. It was freezing cold, as it was Winter time in Oz, but so incredibly peaceful and beautiful. The morning sun rose like a big ball of fire, turning the skies into powdery tones of peach and pink and purple. The colours framed the calm tranquillity of the sea and its lapping waves below. It was like heaven, and I felt so free, so carefree, quite a stark contrast to only a few months ago. 'Wow... Only a few months ago! I thought, as I felt my new freedom in the glow of the rising sun, 'How quickly life can change!' - and it felt great!!

My Teacher, Darshana, was German but living in Australia for years. She was about my own height, 5'7", and dressed in beautiful white linen pants and loosely fitting pretty white tunics. She had a calmness about her. Her blue eyes were vibrant and bright, framed by her short shoulder length bleach blonde hair. Her bright white smile seemed tattooed on her face, as though she could wear no frown, and I thought to myself 'how lovely it must be to live a life of peace, such as this'.

Mediation was something I had tried many many times in my life; in fact, I had tried it so many times that eventually I succumbed to the idea that all these Hippies, sitting in the lotus position, must all be telling lies and making up the effects of meditation: I never got it. How do you sit there for an hour without scratching your nose, doing up shopping lists or going through past conversations where you know you could have said something differently? How the hell do you empty your mind? What does that even mean: to empty your mind... surely, I would just keel over and die! As much as that was appealing to me only a few months previously, I was happy now. I had begun to find myself and wasn't handing that over so quickly anymore! It all seemed impossible to me, and although I always wanted the benefits, I never really seemed to get very close to them at all. This time was different though. Something just clicked for me and within just a few short days of practising every single morning on the beach, I was feeling the benefits. I could feel a calmness to myself, to my reactions. I noticed that situations where once I would have felt stressed out, there seemed to be more space and time between the situation and my reaction to it. I seemed to have more time to react calmly: my Ayahuasca calm was getting great support! Perhaps it was my new relationship with myself, my new trust and ability to listen to my inner self, but something just clicked.

When I was leaving Noosa, Darshana offered me to go visit her in India, to meet her Guruji in Rishikesh, where she taught her Meditation. She lived in Oz but travelled to India several times a year and lived between the two countries. I had removed India from my list of places to go this time around, so I told her it was unlikely to happen. Although India had always been somewhere I wanted to go, I knew it was hectic and what I needed now more than anything was calm; I wasn't sure it was a good idea. I told her I would think about it and if it was meant to be, it would all line up and work out. It seemed everything else was doing that right now, the Universe was rewarding me for literally going with the flow. In a strange way I knew, while saying goodbye, that I would see her again. She laughed softly with me, knowing it was true.

***

CHAPTER FOUR

MALAYSIA

It was the end of August, and I waved goodbye to Hobo. The Australia visa never worked out; they never changed the rules while I was there and so it seemed I was too old on this occasion to get a work visa. I took it as another sign from the Universe. I stayed in flow and decided I would leave and go to Southeast Asia. Of course, the fact that Piers was now offering to come to Malaysia, sweetened the sadness of not being able to work in Oz. I decided for my Birthday I would fly to Malaysia and treat myself to the turquoise waters of Langkawi! After Langkawi it was agreed that I would fly back to Kuala Lumper, to meet Piers! Time was flying and we were both excited and nervous about meeting up. We had been in constant contact, at this stage, and neither of us could wait any longer! It had become frustrating to even talk to each other; we were both just so impatient about finally meeting face to face.

Over the past few months Piers had been quizzing me about my likes and dislikes and seemed really into getting to know me. He was keen to impress and even bought my return flight, from Kuala Lumper to Langkawi for me. I was blown away by his generosity. He said he wanted to treat me like a Princess, and as he was still my travel agent, he had the whole trip planned out. He told me, as we would be travelling together, he had gone ahead and made some bookings. The first, he said, was a plush Backpackers Hostel, near the Petronas towers, in the city centre for our first night together. I was well used to camping and hostels at this stage, so a plush hostel sounded amazing to me!

As the time to meet loomed closer, I packed up my rucksack and got ready to leave my Hostel in Langkawi. I had met so many wonderful people there, and had such a chilled-out time. However, I had begun to notice a difference in the communication, over the past few days, with Piers. He seemed more distant, less interested, and even quite sharp and rude on the phone. He would chomp and eat with his mouth open, fart, and talk in a way that was quite distant and cold without care or connection. I felt he was trying to turn me off him. I began to get the feeling he was no longer interested, or perhaps changed his mind on meeting.

Nothing had changed between us, and there was no rhyme or reason for it. My old fears, wounds and emotions began to creep in. I began to question myself, my looks, my personality, my enough-ness and tear myself apart to see what had I done to cause this rejection and these reactions. Then I stopped myself, right then and there. I reminded myself these thoughts were habitual and old. They were not the new me, but the old me. The new me had learned to catch full awareness of when these recycled thoughts, which no longer serve me, would arise. The new me, who was meditating every day now, placed gentle awareness on those old thoughts and allowed them to come and go without attachment or conversation with them. They were old emotions, which served a purpose at one time in my life. Now, I reminded myself, I was a strong single independent woman who was rocking around the globe. I didn't need a man. I had myself and would always have myself. If he didn't like me any longer, or thought I was fat or lost interest or didn't like me anymore, that was his problem. I didn't need him and we could just go our own ways if it didn't work.

A few weeks previous, we had had an open conversation already, about what we would do if it didn't work out between us. We both agreed we were grown adults and there was three ways it would work out. 1) We would meet and fall mad head over heels for each other; but we would respect this trip around the world needed to have no strings attached until I got home. He knew I needed to be single and wanted to be free. 2) We would meet up, not get on and go our own ways. 3) We would meet up, get on, and not be into each other, but could have a laugh and fun anyway. So, we had had the conversation, I just wasn't expecting to be rejected before we even met.

I had decided to call him on his BS only a few days before we were due to meet, on the night of my birthday. I was taking life by the horns now, and was honouring myself. I had learned a lot over the past few months and could feel my strength. He was rude, off, not bothered and quite cool and I gave him the option of calling the whole thing off, before he came out, to save us both the hardship. He softened and mellowed a bit, but was still quite cool and not bothered with me. I had originally wanted to get two separate or adjoining rooms in the Hostel, just in case we didn't get on and so he wasn't expecting to fool around straight away. I was still newly single and afraid that my past sex issues would return. He had booked a single room, telling me we could put a pillow between us… Yea Right! So, when he was being cold, I asked him could he go ahead and book a separate room each, as

I felt it might help the situation a bit. Perhaps it would take the pressure off. He seemed more riled up at that idea. He got annoyed with me, asking me did I want him to cancel the whole thing! I felt overwhelmed by his over-reaction and wasn't sure where all of this was coming from. So, I decided to just leave things as they were and see how it all turned out, without getting worked up. 'Ayahuasca Calm Debs, Ayahuasca Calm!', I thought!

As I was saying goodbye to Langkawi, its beautiful tropical waters and all the new friends I had made, leaving to catch my flight to KL, my phone beeped. It was a message from Piers. He was to send me over the address for our hostel, that morning, so I knew where to go. The Hostel where I was to meet him later that evening. His flight was due in at 11pm, so only a few hours and we would finally meet each other! I read the message which said: 'Surprise Darlin! We are booked to stay at the 5* Shangri-La Hotel, KL. You are to check in, go to the room, relax, use the facilities... then I'll see you real soon - XX'. I was blown away... Firstly he was all cute and sweet again, so clearly the cold shoulder had thawed out and secondly....OMG! A 5*Hotel! No more hostels for me! What a sweetheart!

I decided to catch a cab from the Airport to the Hotel; after all I was going to be staying in 5* luxury so I thought I'd splash out! The Hotel was stunning. However, when my dusty, battered, backpack was taken by the Doorman, I felt a little underdressed and so scruffy, in my hiking boots, denim shorts and tight white vest top! It was clear my budget was far below this Hotel! I checked in and was brought straight to the room by my 'Experience Manager'. The room had its own doorbell. He opened the door and as he led me in, I saw the bed covered with roses in a heart shape! He looked sweetly at me and congratulated me on our wedding! I was mortified! I had forgotten, in Malaysia, they are quite traditional. Couples showing any kind of PDA (public displays of affection), let alone sleep in a room as a unmarried ,with another person – and for me I hadn't even met that person yet!! – well that was a No, No. Needless to say, I thanked him and sent him on his merry way!

The room was huge and had a bird's eye view of the high-rise city around us. I looked at the bed of rose petals again, wondering whether it had been arranged by Piers or whether the Hotel did it for us, for our 'wedding night'! Either way it was beautiful and I was absolutely wooed. Then as I settled myself into the room, and had a look around, I noticed there was a Bouquet of Lilies on the sideboard. There was also a slate with freshly dipped chocolate strawberries. 'Wow', I thought, 5* attention to detail; the hotel must have done all this because they thought we were married... Hilarious!'. A few minutes later the 'Doorbell' rang, and I opened it to a man holding a tray with a beverage on it. I thanked him, had a sip, and realised it tasted like Mojito. 'That's mad' I thought, that they would give you a free alcoholic drink like a Mojito on arrival. And, my favourite cocktail too!'. As I supped my drink and surveyed the grandeur of our room, it hit me.... 'No way!', I thought. Piers had been asking tons of questions over the last few weeks and this was all him! He knew I loved lilies, that Mojito was my favourite alcohol drink and I love strawberries and chocolate!', I was blown away. All of a sudden, I felt both panic and excitement, 'OMG... This guy is pretty amazing!'. I don't believe any man had ever been as thoughtful, forward planning, and attentive to me, in my whole life! I was absolutely floored and could feel myself fall a little further for him.

I went for a dip in the pool to distract myself for a few hours. By then it just after 10pm and I knew that Piers would be landing and then arriving any minute. The reality had start to set in and the butterflies in my stomach had turned to tennis balls in a washing machine! I was sitting in the bedroom, when my phone beeped…. It was Piers… He had landed! SHHHITTTT!!! OMG! This was really happening. I wanted to jump up and down in the room, squeak with excitement and have several chats with myself to calm the hell down! Reminding myself that we may not have any chemistry when we meet, I needed to check in to reality a little. This went on for what seemed to be an eternity, as Piers messaged every few minutes to say he was a little closer, just got a cab, just got to the hotel.

Then….   DIIIIING   DOOOOONG! OOOOMMMMMGGGGGGGGGG!!!! He was at the door…. OMG!! He was actually at the door…. 'Calm the hell down Debs! JUST CALM DOWN!!!!!'. I shook myself. So, I took a few deep breaths, put down my laptop (where I had been posting photos to my social media account as a distraction!), and I approached the door. I opened it back… and there he was!

There was Piers… standing there in front of me, finally, in person, no screen between us, no head and shoulders shot, I realised we were finally seeing each other head to toe…. There he was, his whole body. It was crazy! Wow! He was exactly as I had seen him on screen, handsome with brown tousled hair and a glint in his eyes, so steely blue you could swim in them. He had a confident cheeky grin, with just a hint of unsureness about himself hidden behind. Seeing him in real life, the whole person, I could immediately see he had a cheeky swagger that matched his grin. He was just a little shorter than I expected, but I felt immediate chemistry with him straight away.

'Aw'rite?', he said as though he'd known me forever, casually with his cheeky English accent and that glint in his eyes now coming alive. We leaned into have a peck on the cheek, I felt shy all of a sudden. He came in with his rucksack, a little rushed still from all the go go go of travel, and immediately went for a shower to freshen up. When settled he came back and sat back down at the table by the window, it was now dark out, but the view was stunning with all the high-rise buildings around us lit up like Christmas trees! It was quite romantic to be honest. The doorbell went, and there was a man with an Ice Bucket and two glasses, another surprise... Piers proceeded to take out a Bottle of Champagne from his bag: he had carried it with him all the way! How sweet, I thought. But it didn't stop there... he had also brought a bottle of 'Chatteneuf De Pape'- one of my favourite red wines, and a little voucher book filled with kisses, cuddles, long distance phone calls and more lovely requests. All which I was intended for use on our travels, and for after when he went home. I wanted to explode with all the attention to detail. He had really put a huge amount of thought into the whole thing and I was lost for words. If I hadn't already felt as though I had fallen in love with him before, I would have fallen in love with him right then and there all over again, and I did. I knew he was a truly special soul. I wondered how the heck our stars aligned to find each other given the distance back home; me being from Dublin and him being from the UK. My mind raced to how we could make all this work in the future, but once again I brought myself back to reality. I needed to keep my feet on the ground. It was easy to fall for somebody and be wooed, but we still had to get to know each other, and I still had a whole world with no strings attached to travel.

I also reminded myself that fairy tales don't always live happily ever after, which thanks to Disney our minds have been corrupted into believing they do! Not all stories are unicorns, rainbows, and happy endings... I reminded myself that it was easy to fall in love, it was easy to fall out of love (I had witnessed it before, in my own relationships and through the relationships I had grown up with) but it was not always as easy to stay in love, that's what nobody tells you! I firmly believe that we have been shown the happy honeymoon start, the happy ending but all the stuff in between... that's what counts, where we become complacent and normalised, where love is most needed. It is the difficulties and challenges we face in the journey together which defines love. It is living in a conscious state of giving and receiving love, which is the most challenging part. It's the persistence by both people to keep a relationship alive, new, fun, joyful, loving, romantic, respectful, honest, and passionate: that is the hardest part. It's meeting the difficulties with love, loving the most difficult aspects of both your own self and that of the other. That's the part that counts more than everything else. I reminded myself to marinate in the moment, but not let it cloud me with rose tinted glasses. I was determined not to get hurt again.

It was incredible how normal and natural it all felt between us. It was as though we had just seen each other a few days ago, when in fact we had never met in person before. I felt immediately attracted to him and could feel my face warm a little, as we spoke. Having chatted for hours we turned in for the night, to our King size bed, and it all made sense as to why asking for two rooms had frustrated him so much. It was a 5* Hotel, so having one room was a big deal... let alone two! We joked and laughed about my thinking we were staying in a Hostel, and he laughed at the idea of us sleeping in separate rooms, while cheekily saying 'You know we would have ended up in the same bed anyway!'. Needless to say, there was no pillow needed between us for the night. What was interesting was every night we were together, I slept like a baby, when usually it takes me some time to adjust sleeping in a bed with somebody new. I usually don't sleep straight away, but with Piers I did.

***

CHAPTER FIVE

OLD HABITS DIE HARD

A few days later we made our way to the Mossy Forest in the Cameron Highlands. Piers knew I loved trees and even more so, mossy trees, so I was in heaven! We had great fun but after a few days I felt friction once again with him. This was new territory, I felt I was being honest and in touch with myself, yet I wasn't sure whether I was reading him correctly. In many ways we were just getting to know each other all over again. Getting to know each other's traits, 'isms, sarcasm, frustrations and quirks is very different in person than via email or text, and even video.

I also felt my mood had dropped a little, as we had been having some little conflicts. I wondered whether it was me picking up on his stuff, or was it my own. I was new to the whole concept of trusting my inner voice, and in my own company I seemed to have nailed it. But now I was with somebody else. This was always where I became more confused. I had lived a lifetime looking at myself, trying to find my flaws, through other people's eyes so I might avoid them, and in turn avoid rejection. My work always seemed to come from interpersonal relationships - and here I was. I was confused on how to read the reactions we were having together, to separate my energy from his.

I felt less content and happy in myself, which was strange. Since I had been travelling, I felt elated, joyful, light and the happiest I had been in years. Although I had been learning to be more mindful and aware of my thoughts, there was still a lot of practice to put in place before I could override some previously hardwired programmes from my past. My default setting up to that point in life was when it came to breakdown of relationships of any sort, it was safer to assume I was the cause than even imagine for a moment the other person could have called it wrong. It was easier to assume it was something I was doing wrong. I was aware of the depths that noticing my mood being low could take me; it was a slippery slope of self-blame and not an easy one to crawl up from.

As soon as I started to blame myself for these small clashes with each other, I began to hate that part of me. Then I would hate, hating that part of me. Then I would continue to hate, hating that part, and layered on the hate, that I was in this place all over again. This led me to more self-hate and so it comes full circle. Still with me? Of course, the fact that somebody else would see me locked into such a grotesque state, made it all the worse; like a monster who doesn't want their face to be seen, I would act out, projecting my fear, pain, misery, and all this inner disgust, outwardly. This in turn would leave the other person confused. A further breakdown of the relationship then becomes a self-fulfilling prophecy, of their not accepting, liking or wanting to be around me…. Of course, this led to me not wanting to be around myself either. I would cause them, and me so, much pain. Then I was back into the cycle once more.

When this happened, I felt so powerless to reverse or change it. This made it impossible for me to climb out of the hole. Because to climb out of the hole would mean I would first have to forgive myself, for putting myself in there. While in that vicious cycle, I would hate myself far too much to let myself off the hook. I could sense the destruction I was causing like a wildfire, spreading to every corner creating devastating uncontrollable damage. It's always during these cycles my friend, the Darkness, waited for me with a tapping foot. A taping foot, as if to say: 'Do you give up yet? You know it's never going to change and you are always going to ruin everything? Sooner or later, others will always see this ugly side of you; you can't escape, you can't change, you can't hide it, it's gross. You can't fix this so you may as well be alone. They will leave once they see this side of you. You've already ruined it now; it's all tainted and so you better call it quits before they do; get out while you can before they get out. They are going to leave anyway, so why not take control of at least something, and call it quits yourself? Save yourself the pain of them rejecting you. Reject them first. You will never be enough'. The Darkness was always insistent! Yet there was a new part of me that had become aware of this now. There was a stronger part of me who had grown so much in the last number of months. But the battle was now on between the newer, freer, stronger more authentic version of myself and the grip and habits of my old ways.

So here I was, in a beautiful country with a boy I really liked, clashing heads over stupid small things and taking full ownership of the situation, once again. I was blaming all the little head clashes we were having on myself. The more I did this, the more my mood dropped. The more my mood dropped the harder I found it to come out of a sulk or to give in to myself, or him when we fell out. I felt uncontrollable emotional flashbacks to my past and it was as though I reverted right back to old ways. We continued to have little fall outs here and there. It was as though we didn't even like being around each other anymore, and I didn't blame him. He wanted to be away from me and I wanted to be away from me too. There was no way to win! He stopped making an effort to communicate with me in any caring manner, it all became functional, as though he hated being around me. Which fulfilled part of the cycle of this wild fire in my mind. Because I hated being around me. I just wanted it all to stop. I wanted out; I was destructive. I wanted all the emotion to end and to be free of it all. I felt like a drunk in a China Shop, trashing the place uncontrollably, and the more I tried to stop it the more I trashed the place. Once it started I couldn't seem to stop it. I began to feel insecure in myself. I began to lose myself. I was embarrassed. Yet there was still an aspect of me who was questioning, perhaps it wasn't all me? He had been funny with me just before he came out, and then was all fine. I don't feel I imagined that. Yet here we were again. I had felt he was being awkward and a little difficult. Instead of seeing that for what it was, I assumed it was because of me, my fault.

But the Darkness was winning, and I was already in too deep. I felt I was messing it all up again. I could feel the hatred for myself. I could feel that darkness wash over me, for ruining it all; for ruining our chances, for ruining his holiday. For ruining the memories of this trip, for ruining any likelihood that he would still like, accept, be interested, or any way be attracted to me when he saw the real me. The stronger version I had become was now fading away, falling into the groove of old tracks. I was trading myself off once more, seeing the real me, being this ugly gargoyle of self-hatred. I was playing old records, well-worn in their groove. My Meditation and Ayahuasca Calm was now lost in the darkness of my mind. My records played and sang about things which were invisible and which I never seemed to be able to fix in myself. These records played out, stuck on the default last track which was to prepare me for total destruction by sabotaging it all, before it comes to a natural end; taking control of the ending, so you cannot be hurt; to create the ending so you don't have to wait for it to happen by surprise. You've messed it all up, it will come to an end, and the only way out is to end it yourself. It repeated over and over to me. I was being tormented in my head. Why was this happening to me again, why do I ruin everything I thought?

I got it all wrong again, I was ruining it and sure he would want to be anywhere else but with me. God knows I wanted to be anywhere else but with me! But anywhere I go, there I am, and so there was no escape. I needed to end the intensity of this destruction that I felt I was causing. I didn't like this feeling. Just days ago, I had a home run of contentedness and darkness had become a stranger. I felt I had turned a corner and perhaps had left those days behind. I had done Ayahuasca, had been meditating and was quietly elated in my ability to transcend those dark feelings when they arose. But here they were, back again, and the disappointment of their return catastrophised and ruined all hope I had previously won. It made me feel like a fraud, as though I had tricked myself into thinking I had finally pushed forward from that place. As though I had finally 'fixed' myself. The broken lenses were back, and the view was shattered. I felt perhaps we might be best to go our own ways. It made me sad, but I didn't see the point in his three-week holiday being completely ruined by our clashing heads over simple little things, over and over again. I needed to go back to feeling empowered, and all I knew was this situation was making me feel disempowered.

The next leg of our journey was to the Perhenthian Islands. I knew he wanted to go there and so that evening, as we lay in our bare empty white walled Hostel room while giving each other the cold shoulder, I suggested we go our own way; that he goes ahead to the islands, and I'll go elsewhere, so as not to ruin his holiday. To my surprise he agreed. He was annoyed at my suggestion also, in a fashion that said he was disappointed in this whole thing. Further and further, I slipped down the rabbit hole. I felt shame and guilt; his capability of seeing me as human had vanished, and I felt only the gargoyle could be seen. I felt hideous. There was no end to the destruction I could cause.

The stress and pressure of it had gotten too much; tears were now welling up and the lump in my throat was ready to burst. We were lying on the bed and ignoring each other. I couldn't cry. It was my own fault. I didn't deserve to cry! I only deserved pain now. I was so painfully sad that I had ruined this whole opportunity. It was a familiar feeling of defeat. The pain was horrendous, and so intense I just wanted it all to be over - to escape myself, to escape this punishment of misery. No matter how much I tried I always seemed to be back here, imposing punishment on myself for messing things up. All I wanted was to love and be loved, not mess things up, and here I was ruining it, right in front of my very own eyes. After all, I really felt that I had fallen for this guy, but I didn't deserve him now. In fact, for him it was a lucky escape, I felt. I was in the grips of some serious self-hatred; nothing could get in my way and the pain of denying myself of him and us, was my punishment. There was almost a sinister pleasure in the cruelness I was imposing on my self. The more mean I was to my self, the better my darkness felt: it was self-perpetuating.

As I lay there beside him on the bed, battling my emotions and fighting back tears I didn't deserve to shed, I tried to distract myself by reading a book. But it was too late; I was running around in circles in my head, beating myself up and marinating in self-hate, I couldn't even read a line. Piers, who had been 'sleeping' to avoid being present in the same room with me, opened his eyes looked up at me impatiently and said 'What's going on?'. I fell apart, crumbled and toppled in on myself crying saying 'I had F***ed it all up, I had ruined it all, and just hated it'. He sat up in the bed, now aware of the intensity of my pain and seeing it all spill out from me uncontrollably. I couldn't hold it in, the dam was burst and I was falling apart. He could see it all now. 'F*** IT', I thought. We are going our own ways now anyway; it's all over, he's seen the ugly parts so he's going to see the messy falling apart -part of me now too. I had nothing more to hide from him. He had witnessed me not being able to hold it together; I was sure he was on the first bus out of there - but he wasn't - he looked at me so softly and compassionately. It was as though he could feel my pain, and in the same instant realised the gravity and weight of those emotions. His softness became stern. He said 'You didn't mess anything up. Everything is fine. We are fine. Everything is okay. Now cheer up and let's have some fun, and the next time you are this hard on yourself I'm going to kiss you senseless.',

This of course made me giggle and laugh. With that giggle and laugh came a lightness; with the lightness I felt I could breathe, with the breath came softness and warmth; with the softness and warmth I felt more relaxed; with the relaxation I felt the weight of such darkness fall away. In moments, with just a little love, compassion, understanding and laughter, it was as though I came back into myself. It was incredible. I felt renewed and as though a slate could be wiped and started once again. I still felt ashamed for what had happened. Although I felt lightness, there was still part of me telling myself I didn't deserve to come out of this yet. There was still part of me telling me that he had seen the ugly side now; it was still only a matter of time before he would leave. There was still echoes of the darkness I had just escaped, reminding me I'd messed things up. I wasn't entirely free yet and I felt my senses scanning him desperately to see whether he was truly okay with me now, or was he still disgusted. This was familiar too. The darkness scanned my external world for any reason it could find to justify my going back there - a facial expression, a cool glance, a hard tone of voice, less compassionate or kind gestures, mean or un-thoughtfulness from him. It was as though my darkness needed to show me validation for its existence, calling me back. I knew that the smallest glitch, which I was hyper aware of in those moments, would lead me back down the garden path to where I had just come from. I knew I needed to battle hard to stay ahead of it. I couldn't allow feelings of shame for what had happened to pull me back in again.

Although I felt him a little hard and cool for all the drama that had unfolded, it wasn't long until we were back flirting and back to normal. Instead of reacting the way I had, I reminded myself that we were still getting to know each other and it was still early days. I reminded myself I was a powerful, confident, strong and independent woman who had travelled halfway around the world to go on a first date with my travel agent, who I had never met. I reminded myself that everything was okay, and even with my mini meltdown, all was not lost. Everything happens for a reason and I told myself 'you are still learning to strengthen your inner guidance'.

***

CHAPTER SIX

HONEST AWARENESS

We arrived in the Perhenthian Islands a few days later, and it was stunning! The golden sands and turquoise waters were fabulous! We were so excited to be back on the beach again. We had rented a little wooden beach hut right on the water's edge.

The day after we arrived, we decided to go kayaking around the island. As a kid I was a water baby and loved the water. When I was in Thailand I learned to dive, and I absolutely loved it. But, for some reason when I haven't been in the water for some time, I always feel just a little apprehensive over getting in. It makes no sense at all really; it's as though I am afraid that I will have forgotten how to swim. It is ridiculous because I can think back to every single time I have felt that way, and within a few minutes of being back in the water, I am fine again. I've gotten pretty good at talking myself over it; however, with Piers there and because he had told me he was such a good swimmer, I felt a little 'out of my depth', pardon the pun. In a way I felt a little embarrassed at my weaknesses and I felt embarrassed that I was feeling anxiety over that. Initially I hid it very well from Piers, but I felt I had become quiet and a just a teeny bit antsy. I was trying to cover up my weaknesses on the inside, by being 'totally fine' on the outside, but it was starting to spill out a little. I tried to push the feelings back and ignore them, to get over them, but I could feel myself become more self-conscious.

My inner critic's voice was getting louder, the closer we got to doing the activity. I was now inside my head and that was a slippery slope in there. The nerves were building and my mind became just a little frantic and chaotic. I was so embarrassed that as a 34-year-old woman who loved to dive, I was admitting that I didn't feel comfortable in the water. He was a total water baby and strong swimmer. I began to picture all the hot attractive diving girls around who were pros in the water, loved the water, had hot bodies and were strong swimmers. Then I saw myself and my pathetic weaknesses and lost all confidence, which didn't help me. Again, I was hiding it well. However, now I felt like I was shrinking inside. There it was again, the hating on myself. Iit got worse the closer we got to kayaking. I could feel it building up like a dam. I was trying too hard to be perfect on the outside. I was trying hard to not look weak, and I was trying hard to show I was easy going. I didn't want to show any drama as I was sure it would scare him away. But it wasn't drama to me, I felt it would be drama to him, because he was so confident in the water he wouldn't understand. I knew if the dam burst and my fear took me over, I would lose all integrity and likely slip down that slippery slope again. I needed some confidence and so I decided to take control of myself and admit to Piers that I wasn't the most comfortable in the water. He seemed surprised and yet totally okay with it, he was very sweet and even said if I was uncomfortable, we could get a life jacket for me. The pressure in the dam lessened. It was interesting how I was learning to speak my truths and for it to be okay. I was becoming comfortable finding myself in being vulnerable and showing that. It was new for me.

I felt this was so sweet. He was being so gentle and compassionate with me and didn't seem to see me as weak, as I had seen me. But where I lessened the pressure, I could feel those self-hating voices in my head again. They were jeering at me 'You're going to wear a life jacket? Like a 4-year-old! Nice move Debs! You will look like a stupid floating pontoon, while the hot attractive bikini bodies walk around looking flawless!'. I began to hate on myself for having the wear a stupid life jacket. This translated as my getting a little tetchy again. He had been sweet and lovely, yet here I was still struggling with the 'I'm not good enough syndrome'. I decided rather than holding back all the negative inner voices, I needed to release myself and be open with Piers again. I needed to practice my communication and vulnerability. I confessed how stupid I felt, for having to wear a life jacket. Although I felt better for having said it, almost immediately I could hear the voices again, 'Nice one Debs, now you look so weak, like you have zero self-confidence! Imagine all the hot attractive women with tons of confidence, you're so pathetic!'. But once again he was reassuring and made me feel okay. His reassurance silenced the voices once again, and my confidence grew.

I just needed to feel I was enough. This guy seemed to be completely unphased by my 'perceived weaknesses'. I was really learning to be present with my inner critics and inner voices. I was learning to let them out instead of holding them in for too long. I was learning to be vulnerable with Piers. I was learning it was okay to feel these feelings, and when I said them out in the open, Piers seemed compassionate.

He had been an outdoor training centre instructor for years, and so had a ton of experience working with people of all ages. People who felt nervous doing activities such as high ropes or climbing walls etc. He had also been a divemaster in Oz, years before. I could feel his experience having worked with people in these areas, nurture and hold space for me. It was sweet to catch a glimpse into what he must have been like working in his job. With this compassion. I felt a little more attracted to him. I felt as though his thoughts were focused more on making me feel comfortable, and less at laughing at my weaknesses. I began to feel liberated and suddenly the vibrant confident me, was back. It was as though she had never left. Just a blip! I felt a little nuts, with these swings from uber-confident and strong in myself, to sad and pathetic, back to confident. It was clear I had a lifetime of old habits to break, and it wasn't going to happen overnight. I was just grateful for the space that Piers seemed able to hold for me.

Kayaking around a whole Island on a teeny-weeny boat seemed a bit of a feat in itself to me. However, with my new sense of adventure and confidence, once we got started, I loved it. Piers had done a lot of Kayaking in the past, so I knew I was in good hands. He sat in the front to steer, and I sat in the back. It was great fun, and I took to it quickly. It had been years since I sat in a boat.

We made it around, to the top of the island, when the current started to change. It became more and more difficult to gain any momentum or forward movement. The waves were very choppy, there was a strong enough breeze coming at us, and it began to toss our little boat around a bit. We were paddling really hard now. It was quite intimidating to be honest, and for a few moments I had images of a battered kayak washed up on the beach, with two missing persons alert out on the island! I know it wasn't funny, but I couldn't help myself from giggling! I guess with fear comes laughter, and I feel I went through all the emotions in a short space of time! I began to giggle to myself at the back of the boat. I had been so nervous about this and here I was in choppy water struggling to row and honestly…. I was having great fun; I was actually still enjoying the experience, despite the images of washed-up kayaks! Sometimes the imagination holds more anxiety than the experience.

We were making way, but my arms were so tired and because my seat was so close to Piers, we kept bashing oars. Of course, in the denial of the difficult situation we found ourselves in, battling the swell and current, I couldn't stop giggling. What was the point in being annoyed or upset, I thought; we were in it now and had to make the most of it! Piers did not find it funny at all, which of course made me laugh even more. Silently I giggled, then panicked, then giggled, then panicked in my head while sitting behind him rowing. Then we saw some land ahead. 'THANK F***!', we both said together in harmony! We had made it half way around the island – Phew!

We pulled in, dropped the kayak on the shore and rewarded our efforts with a fresh coconut and some ice-cream to battle the intense heat. It was well over 30+ degrees Celsius. As we sat there, I felt, despite the whole situation, it was actually quite funny. However, Piers mood seemed dull. He seemed to take it all pretty seriously.

As we sat there, looking out over the calm bay we had pulled into, I noticed how my mood was light and Piers was not. I felt fresh and alive in myself - just how I had been for the months previously. I became aware of how it had been a while since I felt that way, and it made me reflect a little. Sometimes, in a new relationship we can have rose tinted glasses and be so pre-occupied in putting our best self forward, that we don't see the other person fully. I became aware of how Piers was actually quite quiet and reserved, It struck me overall, on our trip, he had actually been quite serious. I hadn't noticed it before, it was as though my new giddiness and laughter in the kayak had shown me it had been far too long since I had laughed like that. In fact, I hadn't laughed like that since we were together. The whole trip had been quite serious. Here I was, away, free, and liberated from all the craziness I had just gone through, it made no sense to me to feel so heavy.

I had been giving myself a hard time, but hadn't realised it wasn't all me. As quite an energetically sensitive and empathetic person, my moods would often match the mood of others. As a kid, when my Dad was in a bad mood the whole house suffered, I would lock myself in my room; it was too infectious. If he was in bad mood, shouting, clanging, and banging everything, firing off his anger to whoever stepped into the firing line, I would privately hate on him. I would hate on him for the fear and intensity of emotions he evoked, and in turn hate on myself for feeling so angry at him. This in turn would mean I'd hate on myself for having no escape and feeling so guilty for all these thoughts. My anger at him would boomerang back on myself. I would feel weak and pathetic; the inner critic would come and down the slope I would go. I would hate feeling so trapped and stuck, trapped in somebody else's moods that weren't my own. I absorbed the emotions and would sink to low levels. Often this is when darkness would come knocking on my door. I just wanted to escape and couldn't. I had felt this all my life. In my later years I learned to sense his mood when it was on the turn, and became adept at catching it right before he lost it. I learned to be one step ahead and became quite good at turning his frown into a smile. The same was also true for positive energy. I was like a sponge. When I was around people who were light at heart, fun loving, spontaneous and playful I would easily match their mood. When I was with anyone who had high energy and enjoyed giddy fun, it was impossible to feel low. It was becoming clear to me; my energy and mood was easily affected by others. There was a merging, and it became to a challenge to understand where I ended and others began. It would take some time for me to learn about energetic boundaries. But right now, I had already begun to see the wood for the trees in this moment with Piers. I could sense the difference, with my new found lightness in spirit. I began to wonder that maybe I had missed something. I had missed seeing how serious Piers was overall. I realised that perhaps it had been his energy which was low, and dragging me down. I felt I needed to explore whether he had a lighter side to him. A more childish free and fun side.

We were only half way around the island and it had been a tough slog. I suggested we just carry the kayak back, cutting through the island on foot. I was pretty wrecked after rowing for my life in the last part and wasn't up for that again. He was also getting pretty frustrated by our oars clashing, which I couldn't help. But Piers assured me it would be easier the rest of the way, the hardest part was over, and the rowing would be fine for the next leg. So, off we went.

I was once again sitting in the back and Piers was in front of me. The seat was horribly uncomfortable, but I never complained. Because of our positioning my oars kept hitting off his again. Now he was getting pretty peed off, and his patience was wearing a little thin with me. However, with my new perspective on moods and energy, I vowed I would turn these serious moments, where we would usually clash heads, into lighter moments. So instead of allowing the situation to be so serious, as we had come accustomed to doing, I began slagging him. When our oars would clash, I would tell him, sarcastically, that I was just giving him 'Paddle Hugs'! Telling him it was my way of being affectionate! This meant, what was an irritation to him now became a joke between us and allowed him to tell me he was going to batter me for all the Paddle Hugs. We were laughing and joking and in no time, having the most fun we had had the whole trip! As we turned the corner, going around the bottom of the island I felt we too had turned a corner, in our relationship. We had humour! I was no longer blaming myself for the seriousness and low moods; I was lightening it with some good old-fashioned sarcastic humour. It seemed to lighten him a little. It also injected a lot of fun, and even more flirting into the trip.

Just toward the end of the kayak trip, when we were nearly back to where we started, Piers and I swapped seats. I had been explaining how the Paddle Hugs were due to the position of my seat behind him, so he decided to paddle from the back where I had originally been. Immediately he complained how awfully uncomfortable the seat had been and how his own paddles kept hitting off mine; a light went off for him, on how peed off he had been at me. He was now realising how really it wasn't my fault at all. We laughed and laughed, it was truly hilarious, and he just said sarcastically, 'Who's F***ing stupid idea was it to go Kayaking?!' It had been one heck of a trip and a fab day; again, we had grown more together and finally we were on the same page.

The three weeks had gone by quickly, and soon it was time to say goodbye. It was heart-breaking to leave each other. We had grown so much together in that short space of time and had learned so much about ourselves. There were plenty more clashes of heads and low moods, but also lots of fun, giggles and laughter. It was clear from early days if anything was to come from this relationship, these three weeks had set a good foundation from which to grow.

We made our way back to KL, to catch our flights. I was heading off to Bali, Indonesia and he was heading home to the UK. It was strange to say goodbye, knowing I had a whole world to travel and yet I was only at the start. I had no idea what lay ahead, whether I would meet somebody else, whether he would meet somebody else, or whether we would meet again or ever see each other again. All I knew was that I had just had a lucky escape in my own life back home.

Our time together had shown me I knew I needed this time alone, single, to find my self and get to know myself a bit better.

I needed this time alone to strengthen my inner knowing and trust in my inner self more. I needed the space and time to become the best version of me, for me. I needed to not be in a relationship to do that, and with all that had happened on our trip together it was clear I still needed to do more work on myself before I could get into anything serious. Piers knew this as we had spoken openly about how my trip needed to be all about me, selfishly, and he didn't want to get in my way. He knew the train wreck I had just crawled out of and he knew I was on a journey of self-discovery. It was liberating to have the ability to be so open and honest with him and for him to be so open and understanding. He told me that when I came 'home from gallivanting the world', he 'would be there for me, regardless of what happens'. I knew we had something special, something which was worth more than we even realised at that point. Yet I needed to allow myself the freedom to move about in the world, unattached, the way I needed to, no strings attached.

We checked ourselves in to the airport and headed toward our own gates, prolonging the goodbyes for as long as possible. I felt a lump form in my throat. I had been holding it back all morning and didn't want to cry. We had both been quiet and tactile in our sadness, as we had travelled to the airport, keeping it together. But now, it was all about to fall apart. As he stood on the travellator to go downstairs, I could see tears in his eyes, but he held it well. I watched him disappear out of sight. My heart wretched, tears flowed, and all I wanted to do was crumble to the ground and fall apart for a few minutes. But I was in the airport and couldn't; I had to hold it together. 'Everyone cries at the airport', I told myself while allowing a few gulping bursts out. I pulled myself together and made my way toward the gate and got back in to backpacking mode. Onward I went toward the next leg of the journey. I was on my own again. My confidence soared and I felt like I had the whole world in my hands.

***

CHAPTER SEVEN

GETTING TO KNOW ME

The next few months were incredible and although my contact with Piers remained, I honoured myself and didn't allow it to distract me too much. We had agreed I needed to go do my thing, and we had had a lot of contact up to that point. So, we decided we would both take a step back, and reduce the amount of messaging and being in touch with each other over the coming months. I needed a certain amount of nothingness to see who I really was. I felt I had gone through a lot of personal growth and transformation in my self. I was more at peace with who I was and felt a deep connection with the Universe, in a way I hadn't felt for years. My excitement and lust for life was back; I felt liberated and ready for some new adventures.

Over the coming months I discovered I had a burning passion for nature, plant medicine, alternative therapies, and traditional healing wisdoms. I discovered that I am absolutely gaga for mossy rainforests, jungle and anywhere I can ramble my way around nature.

On my travels I climbed and trekked some pretty amazing trails, which truly inspired me and filled me up with love. While I was in Australia, I had read a book called 'The Hidden Life of Trees', by Peter Wohlleben, and since then I couldn't look at Trees the same anymore. Now they were incredible beings who had communication and a life of their own; each and every jungle and forest, now took on a new life and meaning.

For years I felt I was a lazy person. At home I just never felt motivated to move my body. I had tried the gym and running. For me, unless you are running to or from something, running never made any sense to me. I loved walking, but felt I never gave it enough attention. Then while I was travelling, I noticed how I was always drawn to my next location based on nature. Be it a jungle, a trek, a forest, or my new favourite…. Volcanos, my next location was always based these! If there was a jungle or a volcano to trek, I was there. It was incredible to remove the self-hating inner narratives of: 'You're so weak and lazy, if other people can gym and exercise then surely you can!', or 'What's wrong with you, you're such a fat lazy slob! You'll always be fat!', or 'Why don't I like exercising; it must mean I'm lazy. Why can't I like exercise the way other people do? There must be something wrong with me'. However, the truth was, I wasn't lazy at all! I was just incredibly unmotivated by the terrain of Ireland. With all the jungles and treks I could get my hands on; I felt a new thirst for life! Moving my body and exercise was a side effect to the joy I felt rambling around these hidden landscapes.

While traveling I decided when I eventually returned home to Ireland, I would keep up this new interest, of rambling around in the forest and finding new routes to walk and hike and trek. Now I knew what made me want to move my body, my plan was to do this at home. However, although Ireland are often known as the Emerald Isle, because of our lush green due to all the rain, the truth is I was disappointed by the lack of green upon returning home. I had never noticed it before; I wasn't looking for it before. I remember the disappointment and realisation of our lack of forests; it was eye-opening, saddening, and it was a huge disappointment! Most of our country are fields and agriculture. Ireland has been decimated for its Oak and woodland through the centuries by the UK invasion, by Europe and the Vikings taking our strong wood to build their churches, boats, and other historical buildings. The truth is, that in mid 2000's, Ireland had a total coverage of 11% woodland and only 2% of that is covered in natural native woodlands. It was said, back in the Middle Ages, that a squirrel could traverse the canopies from North to South without ever touching the ground. At that time, Ireland had thee most woodland cover in all of Europe. Now we have one of the least. Today, our woodland is tiny and very difficult to compare with the diversity, scale, or variation of terrain to other forests, woodlands, and jungles that I've rambled around in. However, although I am less active than I was, I still make every effort to visit and discover what we have, when I can.

In Bali I had wanted to climb its largest active volcano, Mt Agung. Close by it, there was Tulumben, one of the best shipwreck dives in Asia. However, while I was on the island there were serious concerns over Mt Agung erupting. Apparently, it made the national news at home which seemed a little over sensationalised. However, in Bali the locals were only a little concerned; it seemed most of them were pretty chilled about it, at the start. Many of the Backpackers seemed a bit flustered, making sudden plans to travel home and get off the island, but I found it all very exciting. Half the island was closed, including treks up Agung; but that wasn't stopping me; I had to do something adventurous while on the island, especially seeing there was such a fuss about this volcano. I tried to pay a taxi driver to bring me to Tulumben, so I could go diving and see the majestic beast Agung for myself. Nobody would go. It seemed at that point even the locals began to get a little more afraid. I knew there would have to be some way of getting a little closer to the action, so I thought I'd climb Mt Batur instead, which is the next biggest Volcano on the island. I managed to find a Guide who was bringing tourists up, and I was so excited.

We began the trek in the dark, climbing up boulders of old lava rock. Mt Batur was also an active volcano but hadn't erupted since 2000. When we got to the top, after a few hours climb, it was as though I had entered heaven. The morning sky was lit up like a mirror of gold, peach, pink, purple and was divine. Across from me I could see the beast, Agung! There it was, in all its majesty with a tiny plume of smoke coming out from its cone. I don't know what it is about a volcano, but I love the rawness of its power and there's a certain vulnerability you feel in its presence. Knowing it could erupt at any moment and yet feeling safe because you know it won't… but there's always that chance! It's humbling and it reminds me of how insignificant we are to nature; she just roars on and does her own thing regardless of us fleas which live on her back. Having climbed Mt Batur, I wanted more. So, I decided I also would climb Mt Igen, which is another active volcano on the island of Java, Indonesia.

The walk up to it was long and boring, in that there was no clambering or climbing; you walked up on a flat track. There was still some effort involved as it was a long way up, but certainly less adventurous. So, I was surprised with my own disappointment by the lack of challenge. Maybe I wasn't so lazy after all! Mt Igen was a crazy beautiful volcano. It was raw and very active in that there was lots of steam coming out from its core. At the bottom of its crater lay an acid lake, which was stunning. As the sun rose that morning, the colours of the lake changed from pale and dirty blue to a vibrant milky turquoise. It was a bit of a rocky dangerous climb down to get down to the lake. There were huge boulders and rocks in our path, along with huge blow holes with steam, sulphur and other noxious gases blowing out, so we had to be careful. We had to wear gas masks and even they couldn't stop the fumes from burning your mouth, nose, eyes, throat, and lungs. When a hole would blow it was as though you couldn't breathe or see for a few moments until your eyes stopped stinging and watering. You needed to find a direction to face away from the smoke. While making our way down, we passed the locals who worked there carrying huge sacks and baskets of sulphur from the base on the inside of the crater, all the way up, out, and back down the other side. None of them were wearing any masks. I was practically blind from the gases and was only visiting. I couldn't understand how these men were doing this job for hours every day and still looked in reasonably healthy-looking condition. We learned they suffer from terrible respiratory diseases, which makes sense, yet it's the only living they can make. How easy we have life, and take it for granted, I thought. I knew this wouldn't be the last volcano I would climb and, if anything, it had given me a taste for things to come. I had told Piers about my new found passion and he mentioned that perhaps we could climb Mt Acatenango in Guatemala someday together. It seemed like a lovely romantic notion and the idea he would want to see me again for another holiday felt good to me.

Indonesia had so much to see and do. I really loved it there. My favourite place was Ubud. That's a city I could live in, with its ornate traditional Asian style buildings, and its streets filled with smiling happy faces and the smell of incense everywhere. It was so chilled out and relaxing. There was also so much to see and do there: a crafts person's dream! You could eat healthy nutritious rainbow coloured fresh food in the morning; do a woodwork, metalwork, glasswork, or whatever-work class during the day, and then at night enjoy rambling around the streets and bars. I felt as though somebody took all my interests and made it into a city! It was quite remarkable.

I decided rather than just traveling and seeing places, I wanted to really immerse myself in its culture and traditions and healing modalities, but more on a wisdom and natural footing. I wanted my travel to be worth something and for me, knowledge and a connection to nature is the most valuable thing I could take with me from my visits. I had gone on some plant medicine walks while in Ubud and saw there were lots of classes and courses in Massage there too. I had studied the Acupressure in Oz and had an amazing Foot Reflexology session there, so I thought there was no better place to study Foot Reflexology than here in Bali! While I was here, instead of doing a tourist crash course in Massage, I enrolled and did a Certified Foot Reflexology course. I took to Reflexology like a duck to water and got 97% in my exams. I truly loved it and it was as if I had already known how to do it from a past life, it came so naturally.

With Reflexology, I loved the idea that we have an entire map of the body on our feet. We can treat the entire body by simply working on various areas of the feet. I also loved that as most people could reach their own feet, if more people knew about the various points on them, that could help them with day-to-day stuff, then it was a tool I felt I could pass on to others. It became a useful therapy as I travelled the world, showing fellow backpackers' points on their feet which helped them for period pain, headaches, toothaches, backaches, kidney infections, coughs, asthma, hangovers and more. I knew it was no replacement for going to see a doctor, but for common everyday treatments I felt humbled and honoured to be able to help so many people on my travels - and show them how they could help themselves - that was my favourite part. Reflexology came as second nature to me, I felt very intuitive with it, and always loved the surprised look on people's faces when I would point out various stresses or weaknesses I could feel existed in their bodies, and they would confirm my accuracy. It felt magical to pass these small learnings on to others, introducing them to simple but effective ways to help themselves while they too travelled the world. It was lovely to feel useful, and like my newfound wisdom, I had a place and purpose while traveling. It was nice to know I was doing some good, and I felt my learning and sharing was so relevant.

I love growing my knowledge, to learn but also to pass on that wisdom to others. I remembered that moment, when I was clearing out my Dad's office, how I had come to realise just how important it was to pass on our knowledge and wisdom. There is a lifetime of learning in us and as soon as we have passed away, that infinite wisdom is lost. It struck me how the only thing we have to pass on in this world is wisdom. It also struck me how many of us don't have a clue how to help ourselves. We rely on others so much, but what did people do years ago when we didn't have pharmaceuticals? I believed that nature, our own bodies, ancient wisdom, and the passion to share this wisdom held the key.

While working with Ayahuasca in Peru, I had come to learn a lot about various other plant medicines the Shipibo Tribe used for natural cures and dis-ease. Because I had eczema, they wanted to have a go at fixing it while I was there. I have noticed in my life, anytime any health practitioners see my eczema they all want to be the one to heal it, which can be a little frustrating at times to be honest. More often than not, they start something they won't be around to finish and I'm the guinea pig left with it worse than when it started. There is a saying in traditional healing that your dis-ease needs to get worse before it gets better, and every time somebody tried to help I would end up with eczema all over my hands, arms and body. They would be gone, but I'd be stuck with the aftermath. They were keen to try and I was keen to see what they wanted to do. I was in the Amazon and curious to see what natural treatments they would use. They went out into the forest and picked wild plants. I had to drink awful concoctions and steep my hands in a bath of charcoal, tobacco leaves, and other smelly bits and bobs every single day. They also had me.... wait for it.... pick a leaf off a tree, which was covered on the underside with larvae, and then 'crush' them into my hands! I kid you not! It was not the most enjoyable experience I have ever undertaken, not because it caused me any pain, but because I had to squash a load of innocent live larvae to do it! But the Shaman were determined, and also found my squeamish reaction quite amusing!

***

CHAPTER EIGHT

INDIA

After Indonesia I travelled to India. I had decided to go visit Darshana in Rishikesh for some Meditation in the Holy City; it seemed we were to cross paths again. I was only there a month when Mt Agung, back in Indonesia, erupted and caused mayhem with flights, and evacuations. It seems that I missed all the action by only a short window, and couldn't believe how lucky I had been to make it out and get to India. This would not be my last near-miss with a volcano, as I would discover just a few months later in Central America!

The timing to meet up with Darshana seemed to be just right. She was to be there in October through to Christmas. My plan was to stay for a few months. I would do a month of Vipassana, silence and meditation in Rishikesh; then go on to study Ayurvedic Herbology in an Ayurvedic College in Haridwar, only an hour's drive up the road. As India is home to Ayurveda, it would be madness not to study their traditional ways. I was now acquainted with plant medicine, so I found the Herbology side of Ayurveda irresistible.

In Rishikesh I lived in a non-commercial Ashram, where I had private Mediation on the roof every morning and evening. It was truly stunning. On one side, I had the foothills of the Himalayas and on the other I had Mother Ganga, its famous Holy River. In the morning the sun would appear, and peep over the mountains bringing warmth to the cool morning air. In the evenings I would watch the sun set, as a huge glowing ball of fire in the pink evening sky. The setting sun in India, is like nothing I have ever seen before; it was huge and roaring red, and that coupled with people burning bodies, cremating their families on the banks of the Ganga, watching as the fire and smoke burned, I was in a different world.

One of my favourite things about evening Meditation on the roof, was the peace and stillness of the evening transition. When Meditation was over, I would stay behind, sitting alone wrapped up in the handmade Indian shawl, which I had bought in the markets. I would sit in the peace of my world, watching the birds flying home, listening to Kirtan (Indian chanting of Prayers) from the other Ashrams, and feeling the heat of the day subside to a cool dead breeze. I would see the birds swap their day duty to the bats on their night shift. Only 5 minutes would pass from the last bird going home and then the bats would take flight in the night sky. Their swap over was seamless. It was truly magical.

As it was a huge non-commercial ashram I had been invited, as a guest of Darshana, to stay in the private quarter's accommodation of Mataji. She was a beautiful soft elderly Indian woman who spoke not a word of English. She was a devotee of the original owner, the Guru, who set up the ashram which was one of the first Ashrams in Rishikesh. Mataji, who wore long orange robes, with her head covered and just a tiny peep of her snow-white locks to tell her age, seemed as though she could be 30 or perhaps be 100. She had soft skin which was wrinkled; every line telling a unique story of her past. Her eyes were like mirrors and she beamed and oozed love and gratitude. Just being in her presence filled me with calm. Although we had no common language to speak, (I had only learned a few words of Indian before arriving), it was as though we had so much to say.

Every time we met, we she seemed so in love with me, like a grandmother. She held an entire world of softness in her wrinkled old Indian hands, holding them in prayer to acknowledge a hello or goodbye. 'Hari Om' or 'Namaste'. She was now the owner of the Ashram. Half of the long three-story building, which was just room after room of empty living spaces, belonged to her. As her special guest I had my pick of whatever room I wanted; she took me to almost every room in the block. She was like a gatekeeper of a labyrinth. With a metal circle held by string onto her belt, she kept what seemed like a thousand keys, each opening a different door either from the outside or leading through passages to other secret doors, which led to rooms below. It was like a maze. I must have visited 10 rooms, and began to chuckle at myself for the generosity of having my pick. Each room was an empty space, colourful with half and half pink and yellow, green and yellow, or pink and red walls. All the shutters were painted green with yellow, and it was as though I had gotten lost inside a painting, inside a rubix cube. India is such a beautifully colourful country; everything is painted different colours and the Ashram was no different. Eventually we returned to the first room. I had already settled my bags in. It was only a few doors away from her own accommodation and by far the best room, which needed the least amount of cleaning. 'I'll take this one, please if it's okay', I said while using some sort of hand gestures, as though playing charades. She knew what I meant and bowed lovingly to me, and nodded smiling toward her own accommodation, as if to say we are neighbours!

My room, which had a long red painted concrete seat outside it, was on a corridor with a balcony, covered in a wire mesh, and it looked out over the entrance to the Ashram. It faced out over the Ganga and I had an incredible view. My room was humble, dusty and old, with vibrant pink painted walls and those green shutters, with the inlays painted yellow. Over my bed I had a cubby hole carved into the stone wall, where I lit my candles and incense. There were two metal frame beds, with thin foam mattresses, which I pushed together. It was quaint and needed a good bit of a clean-up, but I could do this basic living. I knew I could. There was a second room attached to my bedroom. It was at the back with two large steps down into it. Inside that large open empty room was one little window looking out into the courtyard of the Ashram, out the back. Again with a wire mesh across it. I could see the foothills of the Himalayas further off into the distance behind the accommodation which spanned around the back of the courtyard. Inside this huge room, was a tiny make-shift bathroom which housed, thankfully, a western toilet. There were two big steps up into the room. It was clear the toilet hadn't been used in a very long time and was stained and almost black with grime. I was not looking forward to cleaning that, but I felt better when it was done!

When I went to the toilet, I would have to flip the seat up with my foot to scare away cockroaches - which meant needing to hover over the toilet, rather than the luxury of sitting on it – something I did only once. I had had unexpected surprise visitor while resting and having a pee, when I felt something on my leg and jumped out of my skin! Using the toilet was never a relaxing experience! My shower was a water bucket in the corner, which in turn had a smaller bucket inside that to scoop out and pour the freezing cold water over my body. Needless to say, my month in the Australian Outback without a shower, reassured me that using the bucket would be reserved for only special occasions! It was Wintertime in India, and although the daytime was hot, for the most part my room which was in the shade, was extremely cool so a cold-water shower didn't entice me.

I wore several layers in the night time. I had no bedclothes or pillows so I would wear all my clothes and wrap up in my silk travel anti-bug sleeping bag, with my head on my little backpack at night. I wore a tight snood over my face for fear something would crawl in my ears, nose, or mouth while asleep. I had some cockroach visitors crawl on my bed several nights, which freaked me out thinking they would crawl on me while I was asleep; so, although I loved my stay in the Ashram it was far from comfortable.

My intention for staying at the Ashram and to undertake Vipassana, was to break myself open a little. I had done a lot of work on myself through the years, trying to fix myself, and after working with Ayahuasca I had felt a shift in my self. I wanted to continue the work and knew from my experience with Piers that I had more inner work to do. It had been a long year; there was a lot of pain and sadness, and I needed to find peace within myself. I needed to love myself a little more and I just wanted to feel content, joy and love. It seemed, even with all the time I had had with Piers, that my heart still felt wounded and closed. I was still hating on myself and I needed to find some way of having compassion for who I was and I felt that Vipassana could help.

Essentially a Vipassana retreat is getting up at 5am to meditate, have breakfast and then meditate for another four to five hours, then lunch, then mediate for another four to five hours, then dinner, the meditate and bed. Repeat! It was tough, physically and mentally. It was all done in silence with no communication with others: the idea being it forces you deep into yourself. I was ready for it and ready to be cracked open.

Darshana came to my room to have a chat with me before I started my month of silence. She asked me what I was expecting, and I explained it to her. She laughed and said 'No, No, No Deborah! You don't need to do that! You have been there before; I know by you, that you have spent lifetimes doing this work and there is no need for you to be 'broken open', or for you to subscribe to this type of Vipassana'. I was confused. I had been ready to be broken open and I felt she didn't understand. I needed to be broken open. I needed to melt down and crack open so all I could do was surrender to myself. Once again, I felt I was more deserved of punishment than kindness. I felt she was getting in the way of opportunity to break free of my old habits. She continued: "Deborah, every time we meet, I feel the need to tell you to 'Relax'. It's very strange because I really feel as though you need to know that all you need to do is, Relax! There is nothing more for you to do. I don't know what it is, but I feel that I need to say this to you!"

As soon as she said this, I put my hands to my face and began to laugh; all I could hear was the Frankie Goes to Hollywood song,

'Relax don't do it', in my mind. As I laughed, Darshana laughed too. But as we were laughing together, suddenly as if from nowhere I had a sudden bolt of lightning realisation. My laughter turned to convulsions of tears and crying. I had an instant sudden awareness as though my Dad was in the room, as though he was communicating with me through Darshana, telling me to relax.

I remembered his hypnosis tapes; I remembered all the joking we did and could hear him saying his famous line 'There is nothing whatsoever for you to do, but to Reeeellllllaaaaaxxxx!'. When I was a kid, and even as an adult, we would slag my Dad by this saying this to him. He would complain about something, and we would say 'Just RELLLAAAAAAAXXX Da!' It became a joke. So much so, we even had this saying printed on his headstone. 'There is nothing whatsoever for you to do but to Reeeellllaaaxxxx'. Anyone who had listened to his tapes in the past, and visited his grave, would have understood the relevance. They would surely also hear his voice. Now I could hear him again. It was him; I knew it was and the reason Darshana felt she needed to say it to me, was because he wanted me to know. I was traveling alone at a difficult time in life, and once again he was there to support me. This time instead of saying 'F**K it', he was telling me to relax. So, that's what I did.

My days consisted of 5am and 7pm Meditation. Breakfast, lunch, and dinner were to be at the same Ashram every day. I was instructed to walk with my head down in the streets, so as not to be distracted by those not on the Vipassana path. Darshana had advised me to be aware when people are in Vipassana and practising silence, those who have much work to do feel uncomfortable by this energy, and so will do their best to pull you away from your practice. She said when you meditate your energy is more pure, stronger and higher. It acts like a mirror for others, and it reminds them of the work they have yet to do; it makes them uncomfortable, and they don't like it. It made no sense to me at the start; however, it wasn't long before I realised how true this was.

I would walk, slowly, calmly and peacefully down the streets of Rishikesh and so many people would do their best to pull you out of Vipassana. Many people who come to Rishikesh practice Vipassana, and so when somebody speaks to you there is a universal sign where you place your finger to your lips, as if to say 'Shhh...' and they know you are in silence. Everyone there knows this, and yet it's interesting to see those who go out of their way to pull you out. Remarkable! It reminded me of home; the times that I would go on a diet or give up smoking, and it was only then people would offer you cakes and cigarettes by the bucket load. It was as though they were doing it unconsciously. But now it made sense. My ability to stay in flow and focus made others reflect on themselves and where they were, and thus make them uncomfortable; meaning they wanted you to come back down to their level, to eat cake or smoke a cigarette with them, so they don't have to feel bad about doing it themselves.

During my month in Vipassana I became intensely aware of how quickly we give away our emotions and energy to others. Whenever something really lovely or magical happened, the first thing I wanted to do was go tell somebody and share my excitement with them. The emotions would come; I would feel excitement, love, joy and my heart would beat, and yet as I was in Vipassana I couldn't share with anybody. I would have to hold my excitement inside and simply marinate in it. What an incredible feeling! I had never witnessed that in myself before. I had never witnessed to how quickly we give it all away. When I couldn't share, and was forced to enjoy the excitement all for myself, it was intense. The emotions were incredibly intense. In fact, the more I held onto the emotions of excitement, joy, love, and wonder at beauty, the more intolerable they became. They would well up inside me; fill and course through every vein and vessel with this warmth and intense energy. It would boom in my heart, and I still had to sit with it! There were some occasions I would simply cry because the experience was just so beautiful and humbling. That sounds crazy I know but imagine: the first time you see somebody close to you have a baby; or when you see somebody you love getting married, or you witness a beautiful life event. It brings a tear to your eye; it's just so beautiful and humbling, your emotions have nowhere else to go but seep from your body. In Vipassana, this was my experience. I remember going for a walk where I had been taking in absolutely every branch and tree, and flower, and spider web, and bird, and butterfly. It was all so beautiful. I remember sitting on a rock with the sun beaming down on me, and I just felt absolute bliss. I could feel a smile on my face for no reason; and I realised I had been wearing that same silly contented smile, 24/7 non-stop, now for some time. I cried. I cried at the absolutely beauty of how that felt inside.

The same was true for when I would feel upset, sad, angry, etc. In honesty, even though I had plenty of happy contented moments, even moments of pure bliss; I also experienced feelings of sadness, loneliness, and frustration. Vipassana is not an easy joy ride; it is full of twists, turns and an emotional rollercoaster; however, the rewards are certainly worth the effort. Even in silence the world can upset you, and I also realised how often we share these emotions too soon.

When these emotions come, they build up so quickly and intensely that we want to get them out. We want to get rid of them because they are uncomfortable. However, I noticed that sometimes when I allowed myself to sit with the emotion, not to stop it but allow it to come, to wash over me, soon the intensity of the storm passes. Once the intensity of the initial reaction comes and passes, there is a space where reason and quiet compassion arises. It is in this space that we can see more clearly; we have a better view of the entire situation and can act with more calm awareness. In effect, this has been one of the gifts of Meditation: to allow space and time between the event and my reaction. The gift Vipassana gives is to see that most of the time when we cannot share the pain with another person, when we self soothe and have compassion for our reactions, when we don't impose those reactions onto others, when we don't spread our dis-ease, we can always find a way back to peace and resolve. There is always a way around the pain. However, all of this is also easier said than done.

I have for many years looked at all these well-known Gurus and Teachers - they all seemed so perfect; like their spirituality made them inhuman. This never made sense to me. It confused me, as for years I felt I was 'doing it all wrong', as though I was getting this whole spirituality thing 'wrong'. In my mind, as long as I was imperfect and kept messing up my Meditation, or being a good person, or feeling anger or disgust or lust, then I was never going to get it right.

I remember living with the Shamans in the Amazon, and seeing how they ate meat or fish, and drank wine and jungle beer, and they ate with joy and love. They were not depriving or restricting themselves, except during 'Dieta' (Shamanic diet) when working with the plant medicine; so as not to lower the frequencies and affect the medicine. Food and alcohol were celebrated in moderation. It is well understood that certain foods and drinks, such as meat and alcohol, lower our vibrational energy and frequencies. That's why we didn't have them when working with the medicines. Everything in life is about moderation and it is when we use, in excess, that we see issues. Hippocrates said: 'Let thy food be thy medicine'. In the same way, we would not overdose on any type of medicine, we should not overdose on any type of food. When we take these lower vibrational foods, as an everyday part of our diet, we are lowering our own energy field.

Think of the tuning fork: when you hold two tuning forks and you strike only one, the other tuning fork, without touching it, will pick up on the vibrations and begin to resonate and vibrate at the same pitch and tone of the one you hit. Us, as humans are the same - we are tuning forks! Imagine a time when you went into a room and met somebody in a bad mood: the longer you spend with that person the more of a bad mood you will begin to feel... for no reason? Now, imagine going into a room with somebody who is really happy, excited, and joyful: the longer you are around them the more contagious that is... right?! We as humans, are walking, talking, tuning forks and our emotions and energy affects others. Anything that is living and alive, has energy. Therefore, food has energy: it's what we burn to survive. So, if all food has energy; then different foods will have different energy. Meat and alcohol are foods that have lower energy, and therefore, they are not consumed before ceremonies. These lower energy or lower vibrational foods, when consumed in excess, in turn weaken our immune system and causes inflammation and stress. The Shamans seemed to enjoy these foods, and even found it entertaining that we restricted our diets so much. As humans, we are here to live a balanced human experience on all sides of the spectrum, and the idea is to find balance in whatever way that means for you. For some it will mean no meat, no alcohol, no chocolate, etc. but these are choices we must make individually and for the right reasons. If we were to have a full, all-inclusive spiritual experience, then we would have no need for the body. To me, surely, it is to marry both together in harmony, fully embracing what it is that makes us human and spiritual.

Many Celebrity Gurus and Spiritual Teachers all seem to sell the idea that when we are in a place and state of pure gratitude then our work is done; we no longer feel anger, or sadness, or emotion - just constant happiness all the time. But we are human! Surely our experience in this lifetime is to encompass all emotions. What I feel we are not sold and told, is that even the most highly evolved souls on this planet must experience the full range of emotions. The trick is not to attach to them. So, while we practice being in a state of bliss, gratitude and love, we must also allow for growth. It is in the full range of emotions that we grow, and it is not an accident that we encompass the ability to feel this wide spectrum. I don't believe it was out of cruelty we feel these, but rather for us to be able to experience a state of love.

Without darkness you cannot have light, and with light you cannot have dark. Love and Fear exist, I believe, because we need both sides of the coin to recognise one from the other. If we only had a state of love, then without contrast we would not know how to feel it; and the same is true for the opposite. Therefore, I feel and believe that the most growth comes from having awareness of these emotions, un-attaching to them, allowing them to come and go, have compassion and acceptance, and love for the growth they bring. It is not always easy. As you can see, I struggle a lot with both the light and dark, but I also know that with more practice of being aware of the inner voices in my head, the inner critics, the more I can learn. At one time or another these inner critics served to help and protect me, to stop me from being hurt. But I never demoted them and told them they were no longer needed; instead, I kept them at their post continuing to protect me as only they knew how. How aggressive and angry I can feel at these emotions - and yet they are only doing what they know best!

Vipassana showed me how to be still in myself. It showed me how to own and take responsibility for my emotions, and it showed me that it takes practice, in awareness and compassion, to master the rollercoaster of emotions I experience in my life. Sometimes I forget I have learned these skills; they go abandoned and I fall back into old ways. Sometimes I am ever present and aware, feeling on top of my game and in high spirits, remembering and practising these skills. I am learning, learning, learning, to have more compassion for myself and to be okay with not getting it right all the time.

Once Vipassana was over I didn't want it to end, and I would have been quite contented never having to speak or communicate ever again. But it was time to come back to reality. I waved my goodbyes to my beautiful Indian Mama Mataji, and to my teacher Darshana, and off I went out into the world again, to integrate what I had just learned. It would take months, and perhaps a lifetime for it all to seep in.

***

CHAPTER NINE

THE GIFT

While in India, I read a book called 'The Courage to be Disliked', by Ichiro Kishimi and Fumitake Koga. There are tons of self-help books out there, and to me not many of them change your life, because ultimately you are the only one who can do that. However, what I have come to learn is perspective helps us change our lives. Therefore, a good book which gives perspective, I feel is a good self-help book. This book was essentially about a Youth and a Philosopher who had a casual dialogue between them. Essentially it was discussing life, and how every situation we find ourselves in has a purpose; it may be conscious or unconscious, but essentially there is a goal. If we have a fear or experience emotions which hold us back in life, we need to take a look at what reward we are receiving from that. We need to be honest about it, and this is the way to liberate ourselves from self-destructive habits.

It was this particular book that made me realise how my Dad had hugely high expectations of the world. He had transferred and projected those on to me, and in turn I had spent my life trying to live up to and meet that bar which he had set. It was pretty high and I never realised it at the time. There was always a subconscious narrative with my Dad, where he told me how let down he had been by the world, by his family, and others. In turn, what he was actually saying was: 'I'm telling you how this and that person has hurt me, has offended me, has caused me to feel pain; I'm telling you this, so you don't ever do the same. Please don't let me down the way they have'. This stuck with me, and I could see how my own expectations and disappointments of the world had mirrored his. I was so grateful to that book, to have been able to see that so clearly, as I felt it so strongly when I read it.

It was also in this book where I learned the power of 'The Gift', and because of my experiences in Vipassana, feeling the intensity of emotions and how easily we give and take them, it all made so much more sense. Indulge me for a moment while I ask you a question: if I was to offer you a gift, and you accept the gift, who owns the gift? You do, right? If I was to offer you a gift, and you don't accept the gift, then who owns it? Think about it for a moment…. I repeat… you get offered a gift, but don't accept or want it, and you give it back, then who owns the gift? Answer: the person who offered the gift, right? SO…. here is this scenario… If I was to get angry with you (gift), and you were to accept my anger (gift), then you get to feel just as bad as I do (because you now own the gift!). However, if I was to get angry with you (gift) and you don't accept my anger (gift); you don't engage with it, don't encourage, or indulge in it, don't converse with me in it, you leave the room, you say you're not interested in my projection on you (gift), then who owns the gift (anger)? I do! What's interesting about this, is that when you deal with somebody who is projecting onto you or sharing their misery or negative energy or whatever; if you don't engage or encourage or accept it – putting it politely: they have to marinate in their own misery! It's interesting because that person who keeps projecting their misery onto you, won't like having to sit and marinate in it and so, eventually, they stop their negative behaviour. I've shared this concept with so many people on my travels. One of the first people I shared this with was a girl, on my travels. She had a terrible relationship with her Dad who was quite abusive. She took my advice, read the book, tried out the concept of not entertaining his projections of anger onto her, and eventually he stopped. They have a much better relationship now.

Essentially when we have intense emotions, we usually give them away to somebody, either by getting angry, or offloading your misery on others, or sharing your negative energy with others etc. When we do this, we are offloading and projecting our inner world, our own emotions and upset, our own energies, toward or onto another person: which really, actually is not fair. Now, if the other person accepts your anger, frustration, blame, misery, and pain, then they must hold on to that same energy. It affects them and puts them in a bad mood also. It appears they don't get a choice; they just get dumped on with the other person's misery. However, we always have a choice. In life we always have choices no matter what! In this scenario, if we were to see the process as though we were being handed a gift, we might think twice about whether we accept it or not. We might think carefully about whether we engage in the behaviour by reacting to it or disengage by handing it back and walking away from it. It works. It actually works! During my Vipassana, I realised how quickly we dump all our emotions on others, and it does affect their mood or their energy. Sometimes, we need to ask ourselves where we got our own mood from in the first place? If it was because of somebody else, then perhaps we can replay what happened to see was there another way we could have not reacted the way we did, for a better outcome? It sounds easier said than done, but it is possible and there is a way.

Tony Robbins, says the same thing. He has what is called the 'Crazy 8' which is a trap that we fall into going from depression to anger, and it's like a loop I could resonate with. He essentially says there are six main needs that every person is trying to meet by getting caught up in these anger cycles; ranging from simply feeling the need to be seen as a person, to feeling we have choice and so on.

We live in such a fast-paced world, it's almost impossible to hear ourselves think. The monkey in the cage is non-stop chattering, and for many of us, it's so noisy that we have just become accustomed to the incessant dis-ease and dis-harmony in our minds. It was only while in Vipassana that I truly understood how chaotic and frantic our outside world truly is, and for me it was the importance of finding stillness in

Meditation and practising Mindfulness and Gratitude, as much as possible.

***

CHAPTER TEN

STUDY TIME

After India, as it was Christmas time, I decided to fly home to Ireland to surprise my Mum. I was due to fly back to South America next, via a flight to London, so I thought she would like the surprise. I called her one evening and was chatting on the phone. She assumed I was in India, when in fact I had already touched down in Ireland and was standing at her front door. I rang the doorbell, she excused herself to me on the phone saying she needed to answer the door. When she opened it with the phone still to her ear, I cannot write in words how hilarious the shock and confusion was on her face! She kept looking at the phone and looking at me, until it dawned on her I was standing on her doorstep, right in front of her! Hilarious!!

I stayed for Christmas, it was so good to see Mam and for us to catch up. Although we had stayed in touch and had video chats, I had missed her famous hugs and there was nothing like seeing each other in person. Having some time at home was refreshing and having a toilet I could sit and relax on, coupled with a nice clean hot shower, was heaven! It's amazing how the little, and most basic, creature comforts are what you miss the most!

A week or so later I was jetting off again. This time it was back to South America. As I had a stopover in London, I thought it was a good excuse to visit Piers for a few days, before heading off on the next leg of my journey.

Having some time with Piers and staying with him in his flat in Brighton felt so natural. It was my first time there, in his home; he made me feel so welcome and it felt as though I had been there before. Once again, he had great attention to detail and was all prepared for my visit. He had bought some Chai, as he knew it was now my favourite drink and of course he had a bottle of Chateauneuf du Pape also. We made the most of our few days together and pushed the boat out as much as we could, drinking cocktails and eating gorgeous Indian food (none which could compare with the real deal, but it was a pretty good substitute!). It was all so special. I felt as though it was only yesterday when I saw him in Malaysia and strangely normal to spend time together. It was so good to see him again. But it was also hard because it was clear we had strong feelings for each other and I needed to continue doing my thing. We agreed after this time together, we needed to take a step back again. It was as though each time we took a step back, the feelings intensified.

My next stop was South & Central America. I was starting in Ecuador and Colombia where I was to spend two months living in the mountains of Pasto, doing an Internship in Master Plants, Ethnobotany, Alchemy, Sound and Mayan Cosmology! It was an incredibly intense and fascinating two months! I lived, ate, and breathed alternative healing! I had decided that my adventures needed to continue the theme of knowledge, wisdom, natural healing, self-development, and discovery. At that stage in my trip, I had already learned so much. I had wanted to include as many courses, jungles and volcanos as possible in the time I was away; so, this Internship course in Colombia seemed ideal because of its content and location.

I was in love with this exploration of the mind, body, and soul. Having the opportunity to explore this in various countries as I travelled was humbling and filled me with gratitude. Where others blew their money on sky dives and tourist attractions, I was expanding my consciousness and exploring our connection to spirt and nature. I got to study interesting topics I could never have had the time or opportunity to, at home.

While I was online at home, I began searching for herbal medicine courses, in the various countries I was interested in visiting. As well as this Internship in Colombia, I had also come across an Herbal Medicine Apprenticeship in Scotland. It was run by a well-known and well-respected name in the Herbal Medicine world, in the UK and Ireland. So, of course it intrigued me. The idea I could study herbal medicine all around the world, and perhaps finish off in Scotland which was a little closer to home, interested me hugely.

It was a two-month intensive programme and was only held once a year. The course was a little different, in that it could lead toward studying Herbal Medicine to pursue it as a career if I wanted. This course could be used to skip the Introductory year of many schools, which was an idea I liked. The thought of my studies being functional, practical, as well as fun, was a bonus! The idea that all these studies I was doing around the world, may inadvertently provide me with a platform at the end, was more than I could have hoped for.

The Scottish Apprenticeship students supposedly lived on a farm. They had pretty basic accommodations (which seemed a breeze compared to what I had experienced in the Australian Outback and in India) and had full class sessions all day. There would be day trips, practical work, and a Presentation exam at the end. Its focus was on herbal medicine from the perspective of plant energetics. It seemed to have an ayurvedic-type aspect to it. Given the course I was yet to undergo in Colombia, and the one I had just done in India, along with the Reflexology and Acupressure, I felt the course in Scotland would bring a lot of my learnings together. The fact it was based nearer to home, Ireland, also meant that I was learning Herbal medicine relative to the plants I knew and was familiar in my home climate. Scotland and Ireland have a lot in common: we share a lot of folklore and commonalities in our Celtic roots. I felt it would be criminal to travel all around the world, learning every other country's traditional plant medicine and therapies and not include my own home isles. So, I did everything I could to get onto that course and practically begged to get in.

While in India I had to break my Vipassana to do a phone interview with the course director of the Scottish school. I had to agree to do a 'Pre-Course' coursework. This included 7 modules, which needed hours and hours of study each week to complete, and then be submitted - all of which would have to be done on my travels. It also meant, while on the course in Colombia, (which by itself involved long days of study and homework), I was having to do the additional study for Scotland. It was incredibly intense. But I loved every minute of it and loved the material I was learning about.

My days in the Colombian Internship started early, getting up at 6am for Meditation, Tai-Chi, Qi-gong or some form of mindfulness exercise. Then we had a simple breakfast, then it was on to classwork. We would break for lunch and then have lab work or more lessons in the afternoon. Then later in the evening, we all had a simple dinner together. The evenings were for us, and all of this was for 6 days a week. We had one day off to go into Pasto or do whatever we wanted. As we lived quite far out in the mountains of Pasto, in the middle of nowhere, it was normal that we would stay on site.

There were four others on the course, one from Utah, one from Russia and a couple from Quebec. We lived together on site in a beautiful wooden building. It was cool in the mountains and once again, layers were the fashion of the day! When the sun came out it was stunning. It was truly beautiful there, with the rolling mountain mist in the morning, creeping silently in, then evaporating into the late morning sun. It was heaven. But the study, was hell! Not because of the Colombian course, but because when everyone else had down time to chill out and relax, play, and get to know one another, I had was working hard to complete my homework for the Scottish School too.

After the Internship in Pasto, Colombia, I continued backpacking around the rest of the country. It was stunning. I can safely say Colombia has a forever home in my heart. However, I knew I would be moving around a lot, from hostel to hostel and town to town. This meant I needed to get the Scottish schoolwork done while in Pasto, while I was somewhere static. That meant, every evening and every weekend, at the Internship I was studying and working. The Scottish Schoolwork included learning a lot about energetics, anatomy, physiology and information much more akin to college coursework. However, I found that my study from the Scottish School actually boosted my learning and understanding of the Internship in Colombia. One helped the other, which made sense, but in a way I felt was all more than co-incidence. The Universe was playing with me and showing me that I was on the right path. The Universe is so clever like that! - she always manages to find a way to show me that I am doing the right thing; and for my soul I was loving all there was to learn in these modalities.

For part of the Columbian course, we also underwent a Shamanic Dieta. This was similar to the one I had done for Ayahuasca and to another one I had done while in India in the Ayurvedic College. It meant fasting and working with Master plants. This made studying in the evening and weekends a little more tricky, due to brain fog and distractions. However, all the coursework was incredibly interesting yet intense, and there was a lot of work to be finished for the Scottish school so I could enjoy the rest of my travels.

By the end of my two months, I had submitted all my Scottish schoolwork via email. I decided I would spend the following month after the internship, travelling around the country of Colombia. After that I intended on heading to Central America. I had done the study, now it was time for Volcanos and Forests... Mossy Forests!

***

CHAPTER ELEVEN

OVERWHLEMED

During my time in Colombia, I had kept in contact with Piers. As my travel agent he was still offering some fab advice on where to go, and what to not miss out on. He knew what I liked. Through his advice I managed to visit some really special locations, such colourful Cartagena, Tyrona National Park- where Jungle meets the sea, Salerno- with its huge Palm Trees, San Gil for Paragliding, and Minca in the mountains. It was all spectacular and of all the countries I have visited, Colombia is one I feel I would return to in a heartbeat.

I had mentioned my travel plans to Piers, which included going to Central America, after I was finished exploring Colombia. I started off in Costa Rica to visit the beautiful Monte Verde Cloud Forest - of course! Lots of mossy trees there! While I was in Costa Rica I, very unintentionally and accidentally, ended up living in a big Fig Tree Treehouse! Yes, it was an actual Fig Tree! It had been converted into a Treehouse with an open fronted bedroom.

Which meant, as I lay in bed, it looked out over tree canopies and forest. It was HUGE and incredibly special. I lived there for free. In return I worked on their Medicinal Herbal Farm. Having just studied Herbal Medicine in all these countries, it felt like a dream come true to actually work with the herbs. To help grow them. To work with them up close, get to know more of their medicinal values and learn, learn, learn! The farm had everything labelled, like a botanic garden. It had the medicinal names, their uses, and I can't even describe what a paradise it was, for somebody like me. It was on Central America's largest medicinal herb farm and run by one of the most interesting men I have ever met.

Jimmy was a chilled out bohemian dude, an American in his seventies. Tall and long with long white hair. He was quiet and kept to himself. His demeanour reminded me a lot of Clint Eastwood. He didn't say much but when he did, it packed a punch. He was incredibly generous to me while I was there. He put me up for free in his treehouse, fed me and even brought me to an incredibly fancy restaurant as treat. I guess he saw a little of himself, from his youth, in me. Backpacking the world. Doing this as a solo female, intrigued him too. He liked my courage and tenacity and enjoyed my enthusiasm for Herbal Medicine. We had great chats and discussed the world. He had hung out with people like Jonny Cash and June Carter, drinking around campfires with them. He also told me about a time when he had unknowingly gotten friendly with a guy, while on a job somewhere abroad. They went out for a ride on some motor bikes into the dessert and when his new friend fell off, a load of black armoured vehicles appeared from nowhere. They swooped him up and Jimmy was left behind looking very confused, scratching his head. It transpired his new friend was actually Sadam Hussein's nephew! He also told me about a time when he was on a camp somewhere. He had worked in the army or missionaries, or something like this. There was a little old lady there, who was visiting. She had wanted to visit a local church and Jimmy said he would take her. They dropped by and out from nowhere, to this random church in South Africa somewhere, the Pope dropped by. He was floored how this could happen. He later discovered the little old lady was Ronald Regans Mother. Discovering this paradise and meeting Jimmy was an incredible adventure. One I hadn't planned at all. The Universe was guiding me and I was in flow. Hanging out here by accident was an amazing experience, and a whole other story by itself. Then I moved onto Nicaragua, for more Jungle and Volcano adventures, and my plan was to then move up into Honduras and over to Guatemala.

As I was planning on going to Guatemala, Piers had suggested that perhaps it was time he had another holiday. He asked about coming out to visit me on my travels. To him there was no better excuse to come meet me, than to do the trip we spoke about before: to climb Mt. Acatenango and watch one of the world's most active volcanos erupt: Mt. Fuego.

Fuego was always a volcano I wanted to see! To see her in all her glory - you needed to watch from afar, up high. At night she would erupt and spit out burning red hot molten lava; this meant the best view was by climbing up her sister volcano, Mt Acatenango. Climbing Acatenango, was a steep long and tough hike to the top. It's a popular Backpacker trip, but not for the faint of heart, and certainly not for those who are unfit. It takes a whole day to climb to the top - approx. 10,000ft up. Here you camp at night with Mt Fuego as your backdrop. Hearing her booming and belching, as she erupts off in the distance, and to see her spew her fire at night, would be incredible. I had seen so many photos on my travels from other Backpackers, and through the years at home watching TV; now I just had to do it. I had been training for that moment, unknowingly, with all my trekking and hiking and with my previous volcano trips. Mt Fuego is so active that you are almost guaranteed to see it erupting, spewing out plumes of smoke, molten rock, and lava from its core. To me, there was always something so unique and majestic about volcanos, but Fuego was different. She was active, alive, and the sheer idea that just one wrong eruption and we could all be killed instantly, humbled me and yet thrilled me to the core.

I had been talking about it for months. I was looking forward to the difficult trek, and the excitement of seeing live active lava was thrilling; however, the idea of it also made me feel anxious. I couldn't believe it was a year since myself and Piers had first been introduced to each other. It was half a year from when we had first met. Half a year from when he first suggested that we climb that volcano together. It seemed such a wild idea at the time; I wasn't even sure if it was likely. We hardly knew each other at that stage. Yet here we were making plans together once again - to be travel buddies again - to climb that big ass volcano together!

I felt nervous. I knew by the time I got to Guatemala I would be nearing the end of my travels. I knew this meant if we were meeting up for another holiday, it was pretty likely we were committing to something together. I knew if we were in touch, like how we had been, by the time I got back to Ireland, we were now becoming 'a thing'. We were now making a relationship. The gravity of that hit me like a ton of bricks!

I wasn't sure if I was ready for a relationship. My travels had gone by so quickly and, in many respects, I still felt as though I had just finished with Tom. I only knew home as me and Tom. I had escaped before the 'singleness' had set in. I was returning home a new person, and yet I felt it was quite possible I was coming back in a relationship. I worried that I hadn't grown enough! I worried that I hadn't learned how to not make the same mistakes! I worried that I would not be ready and I would break his heart! I worried I would project all my Tom s**t on him! I worried I wasn't strong enough… and what did that mean anyway! I worried I was running out of time to grow!

What the hell did I think was going to happen? I thought to myself. Did I think we would be pen pals for life? Did I think that we could flirt and talk and plan trips together, feeling how we did, and just stay friends? Did I think that I could avoid another relationship forever? I noticed myself getting a little tetchy about him making plans for 'us'. I felt tetchy at him making plans for a trip and making plans to come see me. It was sweet and I was flattered but I was scared s**tless! I was afraid! I was afraid that I was getting back into a relationship again! I could see me and Tom and the disaster! I could see me and my stupid inability to notice all that was going on under my nose, and a new relationship was threatening to me! Was I ready to test out all the growth I felt I had made on this trip? Was I ready to lose it all if I hadn't? Was I ready to test out this new connection to my inner voice? Was I ready to trust myself? Was I ready to trust somebody else?

My head was in a spin. I wanted to continue to get to know and have fun with this guy I had grown to love. If I loved him surely, I would want to be in a relationship with him? But I wasn't sure whether I was ready for something serious again! Why do I have to get myself in to these situations, I thought?

As he excitedly made suggestions on when he could meet me for Mt Fuego, I was silent in my concerns. I listened to him talking over the phone, lost in my own head with worry and panic; not knowing, at that time, why I felt so insecure and vulnerable; not knowing at that moment, why I was so resistant. It was as though the speed at which he was planning was not allowing me time to breathe. The speed at which he was planning so far ahead into the future was not allowing me to catch up with my own thoughts. I felt swept along by his words; I felt an undertow and current pulling at me: the speed of his planning sweeping me under. I couldn't catch my breath, as I couldn't catch my thoughts. All I knew was I felt trapped... trapped by the lack of space and time in his words... trapped by his determination to move forward... trapped without my having time to let it all sink in... trapped to think. I didn't know what was going on, my head was in a spin. I was confused by the speed and pace of this future planning... planning... and moving forward.

While he threw dates and places and ideas at me, I felt dizzy and confused and bombarded and frustrated! I felt as though I was having that dream of getting married; on the wedding day, when you realise you have made a terrible mistake, but are so far in you can't get out and you panic, because you don't know what to do! Stay or Run! I wanted to run, in my head, but I knew that was an unfounded fear. I was afraid of commitment, I was afraid of being hurt, I was afraid I would repeat all the same mistakes and allow it all to happen again, I was afraid that I would become blind to secret lives and addictions, as I had before. Would I know how to spot it again, if it happened? He smoked weed, had an addictive compulsive personality, and just that alone threatened me. I was afraid that I was getting back into the same thing again! Losing myself to disconnection and escape! Losing myself to somebody who I wasn't enough for! I was afraid that I would hate myself if that happened. I wasn't sure whether I would survive it all a second time. I knew that travel had saved my life on this occasion, but if it happened again, I wasn't sure I'd be so lucky as to have the luxury of travel waiting on my side again. I felt as though the sudden realisation of my travels coming to an end, my going home soon, coupled with the weight of my uncertainty in myself; the weight and pressure of his commitment to move forward, was crushing me.

He became frustrated with me as I seemed awkward and unhelpful to him. He was making suggestions on when to come out to see me, and I was getting annoyed with him by saying: 'I don't know when I'm going to be in Guatemala! What if I want to stay longer in one country, or change plans on where I wanted to go? I have no idea when I will be there!'. He was pushing me and I felt I needed time to allow the idea into my mind, but he was persistent and pushing ahead. He needed to know so he could get time off work and book flights. He needed to know dates, but suddenly, I felt as though he was cornering me. He needed to know now. So, I snapped!

My whole trip had been free and easy, without time constraints or planning too much on where I would be on what date, up to that point. I got annoyed and pointedly said to him: 'You want me to choose a date, months from now, on when I will be in Guatemala!?! You want me to commit to a date now, right now! Can you not wait and give me some time!?'. But he couldn't and got angry with me for my awkwardness.

My frustration at the time seemed logical: he was pressuring me to give an answer, while all I wanted and needed was time. He was giving me no time to sift through my emotions and feel into what was really happening inside my head. I had no time to feel into where this frustration and feeling of being corned was coming from. In my avoidance of the real truth behind my awkwardness - and as he hadn't allowed me time to think - I went with the first frustration I could think of: that he was pressuring me into commitment! But it wasn't commitment to the date in Guatemala that was causing me to react how I did: it was commitment of 'us'. I truly didn't see how awkward I was being at the time; I just felt frustration and I felt hemmed in, as though somebody was trying to take away my freedom. But it wasn't about the trip: it was about everything else but the trip!

We fell out, and Piers hung up! He couldn't understand why I was reacting the way I was, and at the time I couldn't either. He got angry and I felt that I really hurt him. But I was hurting too and he wasn't seeing that; he was too caught up in his own excitement. He couldn't see he was going too fast and freaking me out; I needed to feel more in control, and I needed it all to slow down just a little. I was only getting used to feeling into my own emotions and understanding them. It took space and time for me to really understand them, and it was still a slow process; it wasn't yet automatic for me, and he was moving too fast for me to figure it all out. It was a little like learning a new skill, and you're still a little slow, then somebody else comes along who can do it really quickly and they trample all over you and cannot understand why you're so far behind!

After the call I took some time to contemplate the intensity of emotions that had taken place, on both sides. When I had had some space, and some time to myself to mull over my reactions and the feelings I had felt, that's when it all became clear to me. All I needed was space and time. All I needed was to feel into those emotions, feel in my body where they arose, do some Meditation on that, breathe, be gentle and compassionate with myself, and not slip down the slope of self-hating. I needed to have awareness of all emotions being valid and purposeful. In them highlighting an area to work on, and let them go. I reminded myself that in the present moment nothing at all had happened; the emotions were being caused by a story I was telling myself, which hadn't yet happened. I reminded myself that we could still take things one step at a time, and that regardless of the time left on my travels, it was not all over: I had lots of adventures still to come. I reminded myself that I was not going home the same person who left, and regardless of all that happened with Tom, it was unlikely I would end up in the same situation again.

With a clear mind I messaged him to word out exactly what had happened and to explain that I was feeling a little overwhelmed by it all. I reassured him that, of course I wanted to see him, gave him some dates to work with, and soon we were past all the emotions and excited about planning his trip.

***

CHAPTER TWELVE

'OLD HABITS DIE HARD' - AGAIN

Now we were in planning mode together, I was so excited to see him. I couldn't believe he was coming to see me…. again! I knew he loved travel, but it was really sweet he would spend so much money to fly half way around the world, to come see me so far away. He had booked another 3 weeks off work and by now, his work colleagues were starting to figure out there was something going on with Piers and his client.

Piers told me, after we initially started chatting and before we were to Skype that first time, he asked his boss John if it was okay to talk to me outside of work. I was still his client, and in many ways, he thought it would be frowned upon to start a relationship with a customer. When he asked John what he thought and whether it was acceptable, apparently John's reply was 'Don't ask me mate, I married my customer!'. That was it, he had his answer, and in some weird way when Piers told me Johns' answer, I felt giddy. Was it a sign?

It wasn't long before the months passed and after a few jungle and volcano trips later, he was on his way to meet me in in Leon, Nicaragua. It was so good to see him again and it was so good to be held by somebody.

I remember lying in my hotel bed, in Cartagena, Colombia, feeling so lonely. Although there were people around to talk to, to distract myself with, I realised how important the act of physical touch or contact was with somebody you love; not strangers, but somebody you love and connect with, somebody you share energy with. I remember thinking even the simple 'being' in the presence of somebody you love, how you can feel your energy connect, that's all I wanted. It was in that moment I realised how powerful our energy field is. I could almost feel Piers energy and craved to have it around me; I was abundantly aware of its physical absence. At that point I would have always considered myself as somebody who doesn't do-the-whole 'missing' people, when they are not there, but in those moments, I was missing Piers. So, to have him now physically with me, I was drinking in his presence and marinating in our connection. I didn't want to let him go.

After a good few day of lying on the beach, and reconnecting, we headed to Honduras, which was known as one of the murder capitals of the world. Perhaps that's the case for the large cities and more tourist areas, but certainly in the countryside and less touristy areas we were killed with kindness. The locals were so helpful and we manged to get a lift into town one day on the back of a pick-up truck.

We were staying in a lodge, out of town, near a big forest and lake. It was owned by a Brewery and so we decided to have a few drinks and relax into our new digs. We were chilling out in our bedroom chatting; we had had a lovely few day, and all was going well until Piers asked about what we would do when I got home from traveling?

I had been ignoring that inevitable aspect of travels in my head. I had a few months left yet and I was making the most of every day. Thinking about home and making plans for work and settling back in, to me, meant my travels were coming to an end. I wasn't in that space yet. It's kind of like thinking about going back to work when you are on your holidays: nobody wants to think about the end of an adventure.

Piers had been getting restless in work, and the job had become very stressful. He was having a hard time and had been thinking of changing jobs. He had a fractured relationship with much of his family at home, and like me he only had a small network of friends, most of whom were married with kids. He had nothing to keep him in the UK, and to him the logical conclusion was that, if he was going to move jobs, he may as well move to Ireland and move in with me. What was the point in him starting all over again where he was, when we could start over again together? This was fine, and the idea was fine, and it was something we had very briefly touched on; however, we had never gotten any deeper than a passing comment some months ago.

Before I knew it, Piers was full steam ahead again, making plans and wondering when we could do this. He was planning ahead of when I would get back. Planning how he would pack in his job, stay with some friends, move his stuff over, and was already moved into the house before I had a chance to breathe! Then when I wasn't reacting as he expected, in keeping with his full throttle, full steam ahead, future plans, he got annoyed at me! My initial reaction was stuttered and stammered unsureness of myself, and the situation - and my thoughts! Once again, I had no time to catch my breath; he was going so fast I had barely time to think or catch up with my own thoughts. He was miles ahead, months ahead, and had all the plans made. I was only at the starting line and hadn't even decided for sure when I was coming home from all my travels. I had an idea, but nothing was set in stone. My thoughts were blinded. I was moving at a pace, trying to keep up with him, but he was already so far into the future. I hadn't even left Honduras, in my mind, at that stage! My head felt like it was on backwards and I began to get flustered. I didn't know how to agree because I didn't yet know why I disagreed. He hadn't given me time, and here he was annoyed at me once again! But, from my last experience of getting caught in the undertow and current of his planning, I remembered that feeling of being trapped, that feeling of confusion, that whirlwind of losing my footing in the situation. The feelings were the same as before, and I knew I was feeling all of this because he was marching on while I was catching up. I was aware now and so I communicated this to him.

I explained to him that I felt a little overwhelmed and told him 'I needed a little time to think about all this!'. He didn't understand and once again got annoyed at my not complying with his plans. He was annoyed with my not being immediately on board and even more annoyed for my needing time. This wasn't right to me and it suddenly dawned on me... he clearly had lots of time to think about this at home, in the UK, before he came out to see me. He had clearly run through all the scenarios and details in his mind and worked them all out. He had time to mull them all over. Yes, here he was delivering these refined plans to me and expecting me to be on board straight away, as though I missed the meeting about them... as though I missed the memo!

Here I was almost falling into the cesspit and down the slippery slope of assuming I was wrong for the emotions I was having. To me, in the past, when somebody was annoyed with me it meant that I must have done something wrong. Without question I would take the responsibility and often not know why I had reacted the way I did. Before doing the homework on what was happening, I would automatically blame myself rather than assume I had any rights to feel I was right. I was almost about to throw myself down, toward the darkness of never-ending disappointment with myself for being wrong or awkward, when I took a moment to see what was happening. His emotions were high, which meant he was in a state of fear... why? My emotions were high, which meant I was in a state of fear... why? When both our emotions are in a state of fear, and high, then neither is capable of listening and really hearing the other. I knew something had to change, or this head to head was going to end badly. I took a pause while he was talking, and realised we were both feeling rejected because we both had our own plans, in our own worlds, for our own selves, for our own lives, and right now our worlds were different.

This is something I had begun to learn when in India while reading 'The Courage to be Disliked'. I came to understand that we all have our own worlds. What is right, for me in my world, may not be right for you in yours. What is right for you, in your world, may not be right for me in mine…. and that's completely okay! It is okay for our worlds to be different. As it is okay for two people to have an argument and for both to feel they are right… because in their own world, both 'are' right, and that's okay! There should never be a 'right and wrong', as this concept will inevitably end in tears; it is oppressive and does not allow any room for growth and vulnerability. To make yourself, or another, right or wrong creates a tiered system of hierarchy. It is false, and ego based. We are all equal as humans, and embracing our differences is what makes us different to any other species. While we may have a lot in common with another person, it does not mean we 'are' that person; and so we may disagree or argue, but we must remember we are not trying to correct that person in their world, but perhaps help them understand how you feel in yours.

This is a trap I have often fallen into, myself, while on the quest for finding 'me'. When our individual worlds collide and do not match, it causes friction. Most of the time, as humans, all we want is to be 'seen, heard and understood'; and so rather than adopting the 'I am right, you are wrong' mentality it is better to explain to the person why you are 'feeling' the way you feel. It removes 'accusation' and offers vulnerability. Remember, nobody else can argue with you how you 'feel' but they can argue with what you accuse them of doing. It's easier to say 'I feel this way because....'. Ultimately, our strength lies in our ability to detach from the drama. To check in with how you are feeling, and allow it space, time and compassion before conveying that to the other person. So, with all my newfound learnings I decided to put them into practice and so I called him on his 'plans'!

I said to him: 'It feels as though you've clearly thought this through, planned it all out and have had time with it; now you need to give me the same time to think about it!'. But it was too late: he was miles ahead with his expectations, and the plan had already lived itself out in his mind; he was already there in Ireland and had moved in, and any attempt of my getting in the way of that meant he was annoyed with me!

I had been meditating more and had been practicing feeling into my emotions when they arise. I had been practising giving a breath and space between an incident as it occurred and allowing my brain time to react appropriately. My initial reaction was to be swept away. However, when I took those few breaths and felt into my body: to see was this a familiar feeling? - and if it was, when did I feel it before? and if I could remember, then how did I resolve it? and what did I learn from it? I had remembered this confusion from before, in Cartagena, when he planned to come see me. Therefore, I knew it was simply space and time that I needed.

We lay on the bed, both hurting from yet another head to head. Yet another collision of worlds. I needed time to feel into what he was saying and told him: 'I am not saying No, nor am I disagreeing. I am also not agreeing or saying Yes. I am simply telling you that I need some time to think about what you are proposing. You have clearly thought this through and now I need to do the same'. He seemed to diffuse, albeit in a slightly disgruntled fashion, and so we continued to lie there in silence.

I had left Ireland, newly single, after almost marrying a man I thought I knew, but clearly didn't know. I had fled in search of my Self and for a reason to live. I had not wanted to even imagine going home and ending my travels just yet. Let alone solidify those plans in a matter of moments. Saying yes to living with somebody was a big deal; saying yes to living with somebody who would be moving their entire life to come live in a different country was an even bigger deal. I also knew I would need some time for myself to acclimatise to going home from traveling. I remembered how shocking the thud was the last time I came home from travels in the mid 2000's; it can take a little time to adjust to landing back into the real world again. The fact I would be coming home to a relationship, having left the country just newly single, was a scary thing for me. Of course, there were times I had imagined Piers moving to Dublin and us living together. However, first I wanted to move back home myself. I needed time to land, to acclimatise, and get used to being home. I needed time to integrate the 'new me' at home before anything else would happen. I guess, in many and most ways, I imagined I'd move back home and we would continue to date from the UK, at least for a few months to a year. I decided to explain this to him, and he wasn't at all pleased. His mind had closed down now. He was fed up with his job, he would have to start a new job and thought he would kill two birds with one stone. But he wasn't thinking of me, or what I needed and wanted; in fact, he wasn't having any of it.

I lay on the bed and went through all the scenarios, irritated and frustrated by his inability to look at things from my side, while I looked at it them from his side. I could see and understand how he felt. It made lots of sense, but I also knew how finalised these plans of his made me feel. Before I went travelling, I had been with Tom for years. I had barely any time alone by myself, to establish a sense of solidarity. In many ways, I was still in shock when I had left home. I had hoped, on my return, to find a renewed inner strength in that solidarity and to feel defined and separate from him. In many ways I was terrified of going home without that 'alone time', to integrate the new me. To morph right back into a relationship again scared me. I was afraid I would resent Piers for not giving me that time. I was afraid leaving Ireland, just out of a relationship, and coming home to Ireland, just back into one, would feel like one continuation. I was afraid it would feel like me and Tom ended and me and Piers began. Like my travels were just a blip and didn't even happen.

Especially since I would have had no time alone at home without Piers being there, if he wanted to move over straight away. In many ways the last time I was in Ireland was when I shared my bed with my Fiancé, and now it felt as though my travels were a dream, and I would wake up beside another man. It was strange and impossible to make him understand this. But he wanted it badly, so I decided to give in to it. The way I rationalised it was either it would work out and we would be blissfully happy, or we would fall apart and crumble. My Mum used always say 'If you want to know me, come live with me', and in many ways I guess this would speed up the process. I was 34 and since I had spent most of my life in long term relationships, which lasted for years at a time, I was determined not to do that again. I was not going to wait years to call it quits on a relationship if it wasn't right, and this was probably, in the end, the best way to find out. If we were to live together then we would know, fairly quickly, if it worked or not. So, I gave in and said Yes. It still took me some time, if I am to be completely honest, to feel completely okay with the decision. It wasn't exactly what I wanted and had to give way to his needs over my own, but I guess that's what you have to do in a relationship. I learned to see the positive aspects of it, and mainly the only part that I was left feeling uncomfortable with was that now I definitely knew when I was coming home! Up to now, I had known that I was going to Scotland, and I had nowhere planned yet for after that... but up until that moment, that very moment... I had lived my life reasonably unplanned and had allowed the Universe to flow where the next destination was. I guess the next destination after Scotland was now to be home!

**

CHAPTER THIRTEEN

HAVING THE 'CLIMB' OF OUR LIVES

Another week passed and soon we were in Guatemala. We were ready to reach for the stars and fulfil a joint dream of seeing the magnificent Mt Fuego erupt in all her glory, whilst ascending a big tough-ass climb up Mt Acatenango! We were so excited and, in many ways, it marked an epic turning point in our relationship together. This was a huge climb, and it wouldn't be easy. It would test our fitness, our patience and temperament together, as well as our relationship, which as you know, had its fiery moments. At the same time, I wouldn't have climbed that volcano with anybody else. Piers and I shared a love of adventure and we had grown so much in the last year. All the ups and downs were like the hike we were about to undertake, and the majesty of the eruptions we would experience were like echoes of our growth. If we could do this, we could do anything together.

The morning of the hike we were collected early from our hostel and brought to the shop where the tour started from. We had opted to book our own private guide, rather than going with a group. It was too magical an experience and we wanted it to be just us! I had heard stories about large groups being led up the volcano, herded in droves, and I hated the idea of falling behind or equally being held back if there were others who were too slow. We wanted to enjoy every moment of the climb and go at our own pace. Especially as we had intended to climb Fuego as well. In fact, the only way to do both Volcanos, Acatenango and Fuego, in 24hrs was to hire a private guide. Most tours and guides don't do both volcanos, and most certainly don't climb Fuego itself. Those who do, go as a 2-day trip, not a single, the way we wanted to. But we were stuck on time and wanted to do it all in 24hrs. Of course, this was Piers idea, but I trusted him.

Most people climb Acatenango, but do not climb Fuego itself as its so active. The idea is to watch Fuego from a safe distance on her sister volcano. However, as myself and Piers were adventurous and loved a bit of a challenge, we decided to climb both Volcanos in 24hours. Not something for the faint hearted at all, and not something to be taken lightly. We both wanted to get as close to the action as possible; the idea of standing on a live volcano as it erupted was beyond thrilling and we knew that meant climbing up Fuego to get to her saddle. The saddle is a narrow strip at the peak of one of the ridges near her cone, the part that erupts, only 1km away from where all the action was to happen.

While we sat in the shop and waited for our guide, we were handed some paperwork to complete. Myself and Piers had a read through. Both of us looked at each other with the reality of what we were signing our names to. Essentially it was a disclaimer that said in the eventuality of our death the tour company would not be held responsible. The reality of what we were doing was brought home to us. We knew it was dangerous, but so many people climb Acatenango every day that we thought it must be someway safe. However, as we were also climbing Fuego it meant the risk would have increased exponentially, by climbing a second volcano…. let alone the one the one that was erupting! There was no way around it, and no way to do the trip unless we signed the paperwork, and it was too late to turn back now. We were committed and excited. The paperwork literally said even if our guide was completely negligent and caused our death, that we were the ones who were completely liable for it all. So even though the guide, who was the experienced person on this trip, may be at fault we would have to accept blame. We asked the girl at the desk how often this has come into play, and she looked nervous about giving any reply. I would imagine most people don't read the small print, and this was unusual, so she smiled awkwardly. 'To be honest it's what everyone must do!', she said, which wasn't a good enough reason for us to sign it - but the idea of missing out on seeing Fuego, meant we had no choice. So, we signed our lives away!

Before long, we were on our way into the countryside and up the mountains; climbing higher and higher and higher by road, we had yet to reach the starting point of our climb. I was feeling nervous, and Piers seemed a little quiet in the car also; we were preparing ourselves for what was to come, both excited and anxious at the same time. By all accounts this was not an easy trip, and we began to have that feeling of 'S**t... what the hell have we signed up to!'. But, as Piers always says 'Buy the ticket, take the ride!', we were strapped in and ready for lift off!

Our car pulled into a carpark about half way up the volcano. There was a small country shop and few houses scattered here and there, with a few locals popping their heads out to look at us. I could almost hear them say 'Stupid tourists! Making such crazy climbs to the top of a volcano!': I wasn't sure I disagreed with their looks of bemusement! We were quite literally in the middle of nowhere. Off in the distance we could see the huge volcano we were about to begin climbing. Fuego was nowhere to be seen, no doubt hidden by the majesty of Acatenango's vastness and lying in her shadows on the other side. A way off in the distance on her hillsides, like marching ants, we could see tiny moving dots. They were slipping and sliding down the loose lava gravel. They formed a zigzag and seemed to have a flow to it. Some going up, and some coming down. Those going up, seemed to be sweating, puffing, panting and almost wondering what the hell they had committed to. The others coming down, seemed elated and fulfilled, which gave me reassurance. Yes, it was going to be bloody tough but the rewards were to be huge and the biggest I would have ever achieved in reaching to date.

We began the ascent, starting through beautiful hills of grass as the sun shone down and wished us well on our journey. We joined the queue of humans making their way up; everyone was silent and working on their rhythm. Soon, the rhythm became soothing and almost meditative as we left the steep grassy lands, for the thick loose unstructured and unforgiving sliding lava gravel.

The gravel was, essentially, tiny ground up lava rock. It reminded me of how, as kids, we would run up and down the gravel mounds, the local county council had put at the side of the road. They used it for filling potholes. Here I was over 20 years later doing the adult version of the same. We were sinking, slipping, sliding, as we played on the mounds. We would run up and down them and ruin our shoes. Mam would go crazy at us for going home with dust all over them, and pebbles in our socks. There was no structure or support in the loose gravel, and therefore every step meant you would slide back down, two steps up and one back down, one step up, two back!

The climb was unforgiving and slow and just like on the gravel mounds. The lava rock meant for every step up, you were sliding back even more. It was constant and relentless. As soon as we had a rhythm sorted, we would have to inevitably move out of the way to avoid those who were flying back down from their adventure. They were sliding down the volcano like an obstacle course, like a ski slope. They slid and slipped with great speed. The slope was steep, and I could only imagine the lack of footing they had on their way down considering the challenge we were facing going up; it was so tough! This meant dodging flying bodies, while not losing our own footing, falling further back and then getting back into a rhythm as we steeply climbed and climbed.

Every now and again we would stop to take a break, and we would hear either a faint but audible BOOM! way off in the distance, like a bomb going off, or like a huge thunderclap! It was big! Real big! It was huge! We knew it was Fuego!

Once we cleared the loose gravel, we eventually made our way up higher through some forest; it was so beautiful, I was in love! Such a treat! Even more of a treat to be sharing it with somebody I loved and somebody who meant so much to me. It was incredibly romantic, even in our sweaty state! Who would have thought, only months previously, we would be doing this together! My life was so different now!

The cool earthy air and shade of the forest was a welcome break to the midday sun. Piers looked over at me; I was drinking in every single new tree we passed, as though I was falling in love and as though I was seeing forest for the first time. He laughed softly at me; he knew as soon as we came to trees and forest, I was a happy camper! Sweaty faced, he grinned the most soft and caring grin at me. Our gazes melted into one another for a moment, realising we were doing this together.

Melting into each other, and getting lost in each other's eyes, had been something which happened over and over again, from very early on in our relationship. We would quite literally get lost looking at each other. We would talk on video, or when we were together, we would just cuddle up to one another, and gaze silently into each other's eyes. No words, no conversation, just us, lost in each other. When I looked in his eyes it was like I forgot completely about myself, like my body disappeared and as though my soul found itself for a time. It was as though we could hear each other and as though we would have full conversations, simply by looking at each other. No words, yet we had entire conversations. I could feel them in my body and soul. I could feel the conversations and I knew he felt them too. My connection with Piers was something I had never experienced before with any other soul. His steely blue eyes were like swimming pools, and I just wanted to drown and be lost forever in them, with him, getting lost together, forever. It seemed as though time evaporated and stood still; it became unimportant, and when lost in his eyes I felt as though we were flying through the Universe untethered from matter, and yet joined together as one. I could feel his love for me, his wounds, his sadness, his fears and his heart. It felt as though, quite literally, we were one and the same. Just one glance was all that was needed between us, for us to feel all the love and warmth the other had to give.

As we climbed our way up and up and up, our faces embraced each other in the toughest of moments, and carried each other onward and upward. On the way up there was no time for words, our breath was precious and reserved for panting and puffing. We encouraged each other with glances that said, 'That's it, keep going, you're doing great!'. There were birds singing, and trees everywhere - not what I expected - and the views were just stunning! It was incredibly rewarding to see how high we had climbed, and it made the climb all the more interesting. The higher we climbed the more the landscape changed. It was fascinating.

Every break we took we held each other, giving a huge magnetic sweaty embrace, congratulating each other on doing so well, and coaching each other that we could do this; there was more to come, and we could handle it. We made a great team and worked so well together, never leaving the other too far ahead or behind. It was crazy how, in all the clashing of heads we had, when it mattered the most, in these challenging times we worked in tandem together. We were almost synchronized. It was as though we had left all the everyday baggage at the base of the volcano and as we climbed, we worked like clockwork together.

'BOOOOOOOOOOOM'! Oh my God the excitement was building! There she was, Fuego bellowing in the background, reminding us of why we were doing this trek, reminding us she was on the other side! Telling us to keep going! It was louder now, and so we knew we were getting closer and closer to catching a close up of the majestic beast!

The day before while walking around Antigua, the Capital, we could hear her erupting far off in the background. It was barely audible, and you could see the dark plumes of smoke, from a distance. It seemed so far away, and yet here we were 24hrs later, so much closer and not even as close we were going to be. We could hear and almost feel her every burp and belch!

Piers and I looked at each other with recognition, we were living the dream... together! We were doing this... together! How special and magical this was! Even in those sweaty red faced out of breath moments; we were living the dream! We were shattered from the walk, but every BOOM motivated us to keep going! Fuego was calling us!

We climbed further again and the trees got smaller and eventually turned into low scrub and rock. We knew we must be nearing the top. The gravel was gone for the most part, but there were still large boulders to navigate over and the steepness took its toll on our bodies, along with the change in air pressure and oxygen as we climbed.

Being able to start and stop as we pleased, and not being on anyone else's time schedule was heaven. Piers and I were surprisingly fit, as we stopped to allow our own guide to catch up with us on several occasions. The jungles and forests we had trekked while in Honduras had been a great training ground. Our guide was Eduardo, a local who was in his early thirties. He was an experienced climber who had climbed a vast number of volcanos around the world, mostly for fun and sometimes as a guide; he knew Acatenango like the back of his hand but had only climbed Fuego a handful of times. It wasn't often that tourists wanted to do that climb, and he had been excited to go back once again as a tour guide for us. He thought we were a little crazy, doing it all within 24hrs, but he was also up for the challenge.

Evening was fast approaching and after a few hours of hard work we made it to our camp, near the top, just in time for sunset! I'll never forget making it to the camp. Eduardo was up ahead standing on the top of a steep slope. There seemed to be just one more push upward over the boulders and it seemed we could stop climbing. As we were pulling ourselves over one last boulder, we saw what seemed to be a platform made from flattened earth, with sandbags to support to the slope behind from falling down. It was as though the platform had been in wait of our arrival.

As we pulled ourselves over the boulder and into standing position reaching the camp floor, it was like a finishing line in a race; we groaned with relief and excitedly punched our fists and arms into the air, like 'Rocky Balboa'!! We made it! WE MADE IT!!!! Piers and I looked at each other with a look of pride on our faces; we had just spent hours climbing one badass steep volcano and here we were... and the prize? We looked out over the edge of the platform, way off into the distance and there she was....

Standing with integrity and vigour, Fuego! In the sunset! How much more special could you get?!

The sun was setting to tones of pink and purple, with electric peach clouds awash in the sky like fiery brushstrokes. Fuego was situated straight in front of us; it's cone like a magnificent outline sharply defined the landscape. A way off to the left, in the distance, we could also see Mt Agua, another sister volcano. We were in a Trinity of Volcanos amidst the clouds, and I felt like I was in heaven! During the daytime, as it was bright, the eruptions looked more like dark plumes of smoke with small glimpses of the red lava, flickering. It was too bright yet to see the glow of the fire; we knew it was all about the night-time show. Just in front of Fuego we could see the Saddle where we would walk to in the morning. It was the closest physical viewing point to the cone of Fuego.

From a distance the Saddle essentially looked like a long narrow pathway which led toward Fuego and her cone, situated like a razor edge at the very top of a mound beside and near the main volcano. In actual fact, the Saddle was approximately a kilometre away. However, from where we stood it looked pretty darn close, and when the eruptions happened you could see the volcanic matter didn't look far away at all from there. The long narrow pathway seemed to fall away very steeply at the sides with a steep slope left and right, which in turn fell straight down to the base of the volcano - not somewhere you would want to fall down into! We had only just reached the top of Acatenango; were weary and tired but excited, and yet I couldn't imagine that in just a few hours we would need to make our way over there! I knew I would be sore tomorrow!

We knew as soon as the sun was gone and night fell, the dark plumes of the eruptions would turn bright red, and we would see her roaring red lava in all her glory: she was pride of place, magnificent. I couldn't wait to see it, let alone to get so close to it.

As we stood taking in all her glory, BOOOOOOOOOOOOOOOOOOOMMMMMMM!!!!!!!! There it was! HOLY F**K! Loud and Proud!! OMG! It was incredible! I could feel it in my body and it was as though it came from nowhere; then moments later the plumes of smoke would rise, bursting into the sky and spewing out tons of molten hot material. It was beyond every single word you could use in the dictionary, the colours of the sky, the vastness of the world below, and the majesty of this roaring volcano across from us! It was insurmountable!

I was so excited I honestly wanted to pee my pants! I was like a five-year-old on Christmas morning!

I had to call my Mum! Yes, from the top of a Volcano I had phone coverage! I dialled her number, and just as she answered Fuego was erupting again, the excitement was crazy! Mam was completely confused as to what was happening, she knew we had planned to climb a volcano but didn't know we would be calling her from the top! The call came as the eruption began… there was no time to talk!! There was so much to tell her about our adventure so far, yet the most important part was that she needed to see a real live volcano erupting! It took a few minutes for the confusion to subside, when she could make out a tall plume of smoke and a big old volcano in the background! As soon as she realised what she was looking at all we could hear was a lot of 'Ohhs and Ahhs, and Oh Wows', repeated over and over! Even via phone she could feel the awe-someness of it all!

***

CHAPTER FOURTEEN

DID SOMEBODY SAY, 'LAVA BOMB?'

After lots of admiration for our incredible view we got busy putting up our tent, before night set in. Eduardo got busy making dinner. He was tucked away in his little one-man tent, with the door zipped open and rolled back onto the roof, as though he was sitting in a sardine can. He was sat there like a little boy cooking with a saucepan on a neat little gas stove inside his tent in front of his legs. Whatever he was cooking smelled amazing! We were so hungry from the trekking up; we would have eaten anything, and it didn't last long on the plate! The food was absolutely stunning and as a treat he had a lovely hot chocolate for us afterwards. We sat with our warm cups in our hands, as the cool night air crept in, watching on and waiting to the first big firework display of the evening from Fuego. It was fully dark now and we couldn't wait to see the lava in all her glory!

The moon had come out; it seemed full and appropriate for the magic of the evening. Soon lots of cloud crept in, it became cold and began to rain a little. The clouds seemed to hover low over the city below, and as we were so high up it meant we were above the clouds with a clear sky above us. So, beautiful! Although we were worried it might affect our visibility of the eruptions, she gave us a few displays of BOOMING loud belches before the cloud set in. We saw her magnificent red fire spit out high into the sky, only to land on her mass below, showing off her shape in the night sky as the lava covered her cone like a triangle of fire, in the night sky. We were sad the visibility worsened. However, away off in the distance nature was fanning her feathers and had an equally spectacular display for us in store! Above the clouds and in the distance, we could see a thunder and lightning storm with electric forks of purple striking the earth below. This one seemed way off in the distance over what seemed to be Antigua, and then to our surprise another appeared, far off over near Mt. Aqua. We felt like Gods, as we watched this unique display from above. It was getting late and although we were excited and wanted to wait for the cloud to move off so we could see more of Fuego, we needed to get some sleep. We had only four hours to sleep before we had to get up and start the next leg of our adventure, which would be a mission with our already tired and sore bodies!

We snuggled up in the tent, with just a crack of it open so we could look out every time we heard a boom. It was like an alarm clock going off in the background. We would fall asleep and then suddenly hear a BOOM, when of course we had to stick our heads out and take a look. 'Okay, we need to sleep now... we'll be wrecked if we don't', Piers would say. Then a BOOM, and out our two heads stuck again! We couldn't resist looking at her. We had come too far and there was all the time in the world to sleep, how could we miss this!! 'Seriously, we should get some shut eye!', Piers urged as he pulled me in for warmth and we snuggled in to settle for the night.

I was so tired from all the broken sleep and from such a long and physically challenging day of hiking, that my dreams were half real, half sleep. It was as though I was half in and out of sleep. I dreamt there was another big boom; that we were watching the lava fall down her sides while being spewed up into the air. As that happened I dreamt we were about to be killed by the lava! It was falling on us and we were trying to run away and get away from it. I woke up, just as she gave another loud boom. I stuck my head out to see her fire glow and suddenly, I felt frightened. Was that a dream or was it a premonition? Was it a warning? I could still feel the fear in my body, and it stayed with me. Piers stirred and asked what was wrong? I told him about the dream and said I wasn't sure we should go; it felt like I was being given a warning? He told me I was just over tired, had a bad dream, and it would all be fine. I felt there was perhaps some truth in his reassurance, after all my sleep was broken and it was big trip we were about to do. Perhaps I was just nervous, and it was coming out in my dreams. After all, how likely was it that something as catastrophic as that would happen. There are people climbing up here every day? I decided to put it out of my mind; I would get some sleep and see how I felt when I woke up.

It was now 3am, Eduardo woke us to get up. I felt as though I had literally only just fallen asleep, typical! That feeling was still there and I said it to Piers. 'I'm not sure about this, I know it sounds crazy, but that dream seemed very real!' Piers looked at me annoyed and disappointed. He had wanted to do this climb with me and thought I was overreacting. 'Look, do whatever you want to do, but you've come a long way and I think you'll be seriously disappointed!'. His words echoed in my mind, I knew it would haunt me if nothing happened and we were fine. I also knew if something were to happen, I wanted to be with him and couldn't forgive myself if we were apart. I knew I'd regret it, so off I went.

The climb was torture! We were in the pitch black, navigating our way down paths that were not well worn by trekkers, climbing up and down, up and down, over boulders and rock. We eventually made it to the bottom an hour or so later. We were at the base of the crossover but had yet to climb up Fuego! It was steep, rocky, and my body was weak and tired. It wasn't long before I was falling behind. I felt so angry at myself for not being able to push myself. It was as though I was missing a few major batteries and my throat was dry from the altitude. I hadn't realised it had affected me, but I was now incredibly thirsty and battling a headache. On top of that I also had my period, which had been incredibly painful the day before but which I managed to push past. Having a period while climbing a big ass volcano wasn't the most inspiring fun, however climbing two volcanos seemed even less fun now!

After another hour or more we were up the first leg of the journey to the Saddle. I took a break so could see the sun coming up. I felt I was holding the others back as we needed to be at the top for sunrise so we could see the lava properly. I was pulling them all behind and panicking they would miss it because of me. I told them all to go on ahead. 'No way, get up, come on, you're doing great Debs! Let's do this together! I want to stand there together! I want to stand there with you', Piers encouraged me. 'No, I'm dragging everyone behind, you'll miss it all because of me. Just go, I'm actually quite content here!', I said. Piers stood there, on the next ledge above me, and held his hand out. With soft and loving eyes, he looked at me saying 'I'm not doing this without you. Come on', and so I got up with another burst of energy and determination to forge on.

After another 20-30mins of climbing we could see we were almost at the top! We were almost near the Saddle, and just before the sun broke the sky! It was like something from a movie... the colours were divine... glowing yellow, blue, pink, peach, purple, and gold. It was stunning! There was a sense of flying high in the sky like a bird; it was beyond any experience I had ever imagined! We pulled our bodies over the horizon and there we were, we had made it! We were standing on Fuego! Wow!! We excitedly grabbed each other, kissed each other and then shook each other with the excitement!!! We had done it! We had done the two volcanos and we were as close as any human could get to one of the most famous and well-known active volcanos in the world! We had front row tickets and couldn't wait to see her roar! Straight ahead we could see the razor-edge walkway of the Saddle, which connected from where we were, across and over to the cone.

The narrow flat earth path was approximately 2feet width and fell away steeply either side, down a long drop to the bottom of the mountain. There was no shelter from the wind, which was surprisingly strong and gusty, as well as it being almost freezing cold! I couldn't feel my fingers or nose it was so bitter! We looked around at our magnificent views and drank in the glory and beauty of nature. How beautiful the world is and how much of her magnificence goes unseen! While so many in the world slept, we had climbed a volcano. While others slept, we saw the divine creation paint her magic across the landscape in front of it. It was so beautiful and the experience was so overwhelming; we both looked at each other and cried in disbelief. Cried with the beauty. Cried with the pride.

BBBBBBBBBBBBBOOOOOOOOOOOOOOOOOOOOMMMMMM MMM!!!!!!

Her base was like thunder and there she was!! Wow Wow Wow!!! It was louder and more terrifying the closer you were! You could feel it in your chest and for a moment I felt I could feel the earth tremble. We looked around and already there were tons of molten debris in the sky above her. Thank God she was over a kilometre away! The sun was coming up and her smoke and fire glittered in the sky. We were standing, with feet anchored trying to not be blown away with the wind, while watching up close and personal, a live active volcano! How crazy is that, we thought!

I decided I had to ring my Mam again, she would explode! Yes, I actually managed to get phone signal at the top of a volcano!

This has been a running joke ever since. Because there are places in Ireland you still, to this day, cannot get phone signal. But at the top of a volcano in the middle of Guatemala I had perfect coverage!

My fingers were numb and I was afraid my phone would blow away in the wind. It was really incredible to share the experience with my Mam, and what was even more special was the phone I had brought with me while traveling was my Dad's old phone. So, in a way I felt I had them both with me. They had brought me into this world, and never imagined I would have done something as special as this, and I needed them to be part of it. We only stayed on the phone for a few minutes, as it was far too cold and windy. I had literally just hung up the phone when I looked over and another great big plume of smoke, ash, molten rock, lava bombs, and fire blew out from the top.

BBBBBBBBBBBBOOOOOOOOOOOOOOOOOOOOOOOOOOOOO OOOOOMMMMMM!!!

This time it seemed a little bigger and I felt a little unnerved; it had reminded me of my dream and suddenly, I was back in reality. I hid it well, but I honestly felt a little uncomfortable in myself. Some of the lava bombs and rocks had fallen in the area between us, on the saddle, and the volcano in front of us. Still quite a distance away, but the reality of it all became more real. I felt both excited and nervous. The adrenalin was flowing freely now!

Although the chunks and boulders of molten rock and lava looked small in the distance, as they flew effortlessly through the air, they looked like dust or dirt particles in the sky. They looked small, yet you just knew they were huge! These were a few meters wide each, if not bigger, and their distance lessened their enormity. 'If one of those hit you, you'd know all about it', Piers said. I imagined this mass of pliable burning rock smacking us and sticking to us like magnetic fire, burning us to death in a slow and painful way! I snapped myself out. These were thoughts I could have when I was not so close; I didn't want to imagine that reality while I was standing in the front row!

One of the giant molten boulders landed about half way between us and the volcano. Eduardo decided he and his Porters would go check one out. As soon as the last pieces of debris stopped falling, and before the next boom happened, they headed over! Was he frickin crazy?! He ran straight down to the boulder, which seemed to take him ages to get to! It was only when he got closer to it the perspective of what we were dealing with was highlighted. The boulder, which looked smaller from a distance was actually massive, when we saw them stand close by it. Like little boys, they found a branch of a tree and began poking it! You could see the heat of the boulder was pushing them away it was so hot. They had to shield their faces and bodies from its glow. In a matter of seconds, the branch caught fire. Wow! That's hot, we thought!

I began to get a little nervous for them, I was waiting for the next eruption to take place. They were far enough away, in the danger zone, they would have to run fast on the next eruption. Then you could see her blow and a few seconds later we heard the big BOOOOOOMMMMMMM! There she was again; my heart was in my mouth. She blew again and I screamed for them to please come back, it wasn't funny now. Boyish playfulness with the serious possibility of being caught by a massive lava bomb wasn't funny, and from where they were, that was very probable. Where we were stood on the saddle it seemed safe, but then how safe is safe? They got away in time. We had seen the debris blow before the boom and had shouted at them to get moving. They were back, and we watched as lava bombs hit the area they had just stood in. Everyone was so excited at the sheer gravity of it all!!

BBBBBBBBBBBBBBBBOOOOOOOOOOOOOOOOOOOOOOOOO OOOOOOMMMMMMMMMMM!!!!

Another big bellowing baseful blow! This one was HUGE and they seemed to be getting bigger! Exhilarated we watched the rocks fly and spit like fire from her core. I began to notice, it was difficult to tell the size and what direction they were actually flying in; there were so many pieces in all directions. I was pointing at one, talking to Eduardo about this saying: 'that seems like it's getting quite close but it's so hard to tell' and in an instant all I could hear was SHOUTING…

I heard a VERY loud and freaked out 'RUN! RUN! RUN! RUN! RUN!'

He sounded freaked out and panicked. There was no time to think, so we all began to run. The only direction we could go was toward the edge of the saddle!

'LAVA BOMBS!!!!! RUN NOW!!! KEEP RUNNING', Eduardo kept shouting, urging us all to safety!

While we had been busy looking way off into the distance, somehow the lava bombs had also made their way overhead and they were now flying, falling, and thudding, with great dead weight, either side of us on the saddle where we were stood. It was like some apocalyptic movie! I couldn't believe this was happening! I had no time to think! I looked behind and Piers was further back, I shouted desperately at him,

'LAVA BOMBS! COME ON! COME ON!! NOW!! PIERS!!!',

He had only just realised what was happening and began to run for his life! As he ran toward me, a HUGE Lava Bomb fell only a metre away from where he had just stood! He had no idea as it was behind him, and he was busy running! It was as though we were caught in a burning molten rock meteor shower. We had no time to look above or around us, all we could do was run for our lives as far away as possible from where we were, in the only direction we could, to the edge, the way we came up!!!

In just a few seconds, as a group, our running came to a sudden stop, we were at the end of the Saddle, where we had spent all morning climbing up! Before deciding to run down, we all looked up behind us. It seemed as though we had cleared the drop zone. We all stood there…. Breathless…. shocked…. confused from fear and excitement, looking to see where the lava bombs had hit and to see how close we had all just been.

It seemed some of the lava bombs had hit the Saddle and rolled down her steep sides. There had been plenty of drops near where Eduardo and his porters had been poking at one, just moments before, and of course one where Piers and I had just been standing.

That was close! We looked at the angry Fuego, who seemed to scold us for not taking her seriously. We were now! We were taking her very seriously! The fear subsided; the debris in the sky had cleared and our adrenalin turned to exhilarated WOOOPing and cheering! We were all giddy with the closeness of what we had experienced and of course giddy with having avoided a devastating death sentence! My dream had warned me, and I didn't listen, but thankfully we were all okay!

We went back to the Saddle to collect our things. We drank in the beauty and the surrounds for a short time more. It was difficult to leave, but we had to make our way back to camp, there was still a tent to pack up. This meant going back down the side of Fuego, back up Acatenango to camp, which was the most difficult of all climbs, and then head back down Acatenango to her base. At that stage our bodies were well worn, we were hungry, thirsty, and not yet recovered from the altitude and walk the previous day.

After we had breakfast and packed up camp we headed back down toward the base. It would take another few hours to get back down. Slipping and sliding our way, using different muscles in our legs since the day before. By lunchtime we were back in Antigua, and it was as though it was all just a dream!

Thankfully Piers had booked us into our own private accommodation that evening, no hostels for us! It was a luxury, novelty, converted trailer situated in a 5-star accommodation. We had our very own private hot tube as a treat, for our poor aching adrenalin filled bodies, and it was just what we needed! We had discovered muscles neither of us knew existed and so we spent the evening laying in the hot bubbling water, lapping up the last of the sun while sipping some celebratory wine and enjoying the last evening in Guatemala. We were due to leave the next day. Piers would once again be leaving to go home to Brighton and I would be finishing off my travels in Scotland for two months to live on a farm and study herbs. I was nearing the end of my journey and travels away, and it was almost time for me to go home... which meant it was almost time for us to move in together.

At that stage, all our plans had now been finalised. We knew what was to come; we were done with being apart from each other and decided once I arrived home to Ireland, after my stint in Scotland, we would do it. We would move in together. The plan was, I would have a few weeks to myself, some time with Mam, and when I had myself settled, Piers would move over to Ireland. It seemed like a crazy idea, but we were excited. I'm sure to those people who hadn't seen nor heard from me in two years, who may not have even realised myself and Tom were no longer engaged, they would have been wondering what the heck happened!? So much had happened in my time away, traveling. It was almost as though I had been time travelling and just returned from the future. Piers and I had had a whole life together outside of Ireland, away from everyone, and in many ways, he was with me through my whole journey. We had grown so much together in that time.

The plan was; in the two months I was in Scotland, Piers would hand in his notice, move out of his apartment, quit his job, and in effect, pack up his life in the UK. He would stay with some friends on a farm not far from his hometown, and relax until it was time to go. I would drive my car over to him, bundle everything he owned into my hatchback and drive him back to Ireland, which was an adventure, in and of itself. It was so exciting; the idea of not having to say goodbye to each other over and over again. No more seeing each other for short stints, or by video chat or WhatsApp calls at all hours of the day and night to combat time zones; we would get to wake up beside each other, each morning, and start a new life together. We were ready for it, and we were both excited at the new journey we were taking.

***

CHAPTER FIFTEEN

HOME

I n June, after my stint in Scotland, I finally headed home to Ireland. The flight home filled me with nostalgia and humble gratitude, for all that I was so blessed to have been part of on my travels. My mind drifted away, as I looked out the window of the plane through the clouds, as I thought back over my journey to that point.

I had ventured out into the world, alone, a broken and hopeless woman. A woman who had wanted to leave this world. I was sad upon realising just how lost I was and yet the Universe cradled and guided me every step of the way. She opened my heart with Ayahuasca and lifted the veil of BS from my world. She led me unintentionally to studying and working with many many modalities of traditional healing medicine, and spirituality in every country I visited; and she led me to grow and expand in ways I could have never hoped for. I had also met some truly inspirational souls along my way; from Gurus, Teachers, Healers and Shamans to indigenous locals, and backpackers from all over the world, many of whom I remain in contact with today. I never expected to have grown such a beautiful worldwide family of friends; I have never been so grateful for attracting them into my life, some of whom are most certainly my soul family and soul sisters. Especially some of my Herbal Medicine friends, who I made in Scotland – my beautiful Soul Sister Erica, who I feel truly blessed to call my friend. Who I feel we have certainly travelled many lifetimes together and is one of the most beautiful souls I have ever had the pleasure of knowing. Also, the amazing Mally, whose deep heart has such wisdom and strength, I feel so blessed to call her my friend and to be on this crazy journey we call life, with her. I feel inspired and so much love for these women who have forever created an indentation in my heart. These are the women who showed me how to embody my feminine energy. These are the women who I learned it was now safe to trust other women. These are the women who, unknowingly, opened my heart to feel safe in both myself and in their feminine energy. Having struggled with female relationships for so many years since childhood and all the bullying I experienced, it was these women, specifically, who changed my heart. I feel so blessed to have them in my life. They will forever be in my heart and soul, and I look forward to swimming the depths and heights of this wonderful Universe together.

The Universe also brought myself and Piers together, something I will forever be grateful for. I often wonder at times whether my Dad had a hand in that also. In Piers I had met my soulmate, and quite beautifully perhaps even met my 'Twin Flame'. Our journey to that point had been all magical, turbulent, romantic and healing. We very often had been a mirror for each-others self-work, which wasn't always easy but meant growth for us both, something unique to the 'Twin Flame' dynamic.

Twin Flames, for those who have never heard of this term, essentially spend lifetimes searching for each other; they are two halves of the same whole. They understand each other in a way that no other people can; they have telepathy, are intuitively connected, feel as one, and love each other from a place that words cannot describe. When they come together it is usually explosive, their intuition heightens, and they experience a lot of synchronicities, commonalities and even psychic phenomena. Their growth is on turbo; they trigger each other constantly because they are mirroring that which needs to heal. The relationships are intense, passionate and full on. Their mission is to unite and become one again, whether in this life or the next. They can span lifetimes of never meeting, or lifetimes of meeting and separating, meeting and separating until their healing is done. This is what defines the Twin Flame dynamic. They are a mirror to each other, which is painful, but which forces each other to see the parts they have hidden from. These relationships are not always the easiest, but are transformational, and there is a deep connection which cannot be explained. When they finally unite, and have done the work, they can become one and finally end the search for oneness.

I have, on so many occasions, felt as though I was at 'One' with Piers, in ways that I cannot describe. When we look into each other's eyes, time and space evaporates and my heart merges with his. I so often have felt that we are just One person. We make love and are One person. We fight and we are One person. My intuition has heightened to a level beyond my understanding, and I feel we have both grown incredibly in our journey together. I have no doubt this is part of why we found each other. Our meeting was Serendipity in her finest, as under normal circumstances we possibly would have never met considering our location; and had I not been buying my round the world tickets from the UK.

As my plane finally touched down, in Ireland, so did my daydreaming, I was home. Finally! Mam was standing waiting for me with the most beautiful radiant smile, as I walked through the gates of the airport arrivals. There were tears in both our eyes; we hugged and breathed a sigh of relief. Knowing that was the last time we would have to be apart again for some time, came as a comfort. We looked forward to some quality Mammy/ Daughter time together. She had always been my rock, had encouraged me to follow my dreams and go find myself. In truth there was always part of me to discover at home. My Mum and Dad have always been, not only truly amazing parents, but my best friends who encouraged me to think openly and explore all the possibilities of the world, especially my Mum. In the years since my Dad's death she is the reason I finally found myself; with her love and support I finally 'Came Home to Me'. We have grown so much closer together, there is a Mother/Daughter bond which is quite uncanny. We will literally feel and think the same things, at the same time, while not around each other. Often we decide to call or text to say Hello, just because we can sense there's something up. She is the most inspirational woman I know, courageous, defiant, smart, funny, compassionate, giving, caring, thoughtful and loving. There are truly not enough words to honour the beauty of her Soul. She has lifted me up to heights I couldn't have reached alone, and has always allowed me to be who I am. I have been so lucky to have had parents who showered me with love and always allowed me to make my own mistakes, never judged me and always had their arms wide open for my return when I needed to come home. It was an amazing feeling to see my Mum standing there, and although I felt my Dad was missing, I knew he had been with me on my journey, watching it unfold and excited as he had himself loved to travel. My trip to the Outback was my dedication to him.

The past two years had been a whirlwind and I had come back a different version of myself, yet still the same. People ask me 'Did my travels change me', and I answer, 'It didn't change me, it just made me a more authentic version of myself'. I had begun the exciting journey of realising who I was, what I liked, and what I didn't like. I was only at the start, had my training wheels off so to speak, and no doubt I would fall off the wagon at times in the future. However, I also knew I would get back up. I knew that I would forget some lessons, remember, and then re-apply them again until they were my new normal. I was beginning to see the difficulties I had, be present with them and rather than be disappointed when they returned, had compassion, and let them pass. I was stronger and more resilient. I had seen myself for who I was and that was okay. Making mistakes and not being perfect, that's what makes us human. Learning truths and then exchanging and swapping them for new truths, that's what makes us human. Experiencing the full gamut of emotions, that's what makes us human.

I had realised on my travels that sometimes we see the spiritual path as a place or milestone that needs to be reached, a perfect nirvana state that we need to stay consistently in. There are many spiritual teachers and guides in life, however at some point we come to see the glass ceiling and realise that the only person who can take you past that, is yourself. We are spirits having a human experience, and therefore we are meant to know what it means to be human. We are also humans seeking a spiritual experience, and so must ask ourselves why? Where did we come from? And so, we realise that as humans we are constantly searching for our way back home. Sometimes that feeling of being lost can be painful and cause a kind of homesickness, a disconnection with Source. It is our birth right to find that peace in ourselves here, while we live this human experience. This has since become the body of my work. Helping people come home to themselves.

In my time away I had stopped following others and began to follow myself. I had swapped my following the herd, for following my gut. I had begun to listen to my body, to my instinct and trust in myself more. It was difficult; I didn't always get it right but that was okay too, it was all new for me. I began to accept my emotions and sensitivities, and knew they needed more time, but I was seeing them more clearly and with less distain. My self-hating and destructive slippery slopes still appeared from time to time, but I was more present with them and instead of feeling engulfed I would question where I was feeling the pain in my body. I would listen to my inner dialogue and narrative, and I would question where those were coming from? I began to appreciate the communication my body had been making with me, and I began to listen to the little child inside who had been so neglected for years.

I had begun to awaken to the sleep I had been in, hiding behind the older version of myself which no longer served me, and I had dusted off my soul. I had found my voice and regained an inner strength which had been lying dormant, in waiting for years, to be re-discovered.

I had learned many life lessons and musings from the people I met, the studies I did and from all my experiences. While travelling I finally settled into my own greatness and never felt I needed to apologise or explain it to anyone. I no longer had to stuff myself into a box that I had grown out of, but I could stretch my soul and take the shape it had longed for. People seemed to accept and truly see me, for me. It was as though I no longer had to hide. I had never felt as at home in the world as I had while meeting so many beautiful humanbeings on my travels. I realised I am an incredibly perceptive and intuitive being - we all are - we just need the right conditions and environment to grow. I needed to be away from my old life, uninfluenced and untethered, to grow. The inspirational beings I met along my way have inspired my life and touched me in ways that have left indelible wisdom on my soul. I was finally at home in myself, and without effort happened on the right people at the right time. I seemed to learn the right information, at the right time, which then seemed to find its way to the right person at the right time.

I felt as though I had peeled myself back, like the layers of an onion. I hadn't changed, I had just become a more authentic version of myself and owned myself like never before. I no longer gave away my ownership to others. I no longer needed to try and see myself through other people's eyes, to avoid rejection and to be the person I felt at the time they needed me to be. I learned to see the agenda of others more clearly; to see their pain and projections which they had been placing on to me. Instead of absorbing this, I would hand it back to them. I could feel authenticity in real time, without fear. I began to separate my feelings from those of others, understanding who owned what; to de-tangle and become less confused by what I was reading from another, versus what I was feeling in myself: a process which was new to me and confusing. A process which is still imperfect today and may well be for years to come. I began to take responsibility for what was mine and encourage others to see and take responsibility for what was theirs. I began to see the world with a new fresh perspective.

I began to see more clearly, the pain we experience in the world most often has a learning and life lesson. It will happen over and over until we see it for what it is, learn and let go. To let go we must first see it, then we must forgive it in ourselves and allow for our imperfections; then understand how we are all acting out of either love or fear and attracting the answer to our problems by means of creating mirrors in the world. When something causes us to be upset, we should ask inside, not why is this person causing me to feel this way, but what is it about this situation or person which stirs up this reaction in me? Then we can be free. If the lessons come too thick and hard and you find it too intense to be in that relationship or situation, then you have three choices: Change, Remove or Accept. I also came to understand the role of communication in having compassion and vulnerability for yourself. It's not easy to admit your weaknesses and flaws. It's scary to trust another with your weaknesses. To hope they can hold that space. That they can honour and not use or abuse that trust, and it's okay to admit your are not perfect. It's okay to ask for help, and it's okay to communicate your needs. That's how we grow, with the love, support and trust of those we share our journey with. It is an honour to be on this journey with such amazing souls.

On my travels I had also come to understand what is right in my world may not be right in another person's world, and that's okay. I learned that our worlds don't need to match, and if they differ and the other person disagrees, that it okay too. It doesn't mean I am wrong; it just means in their world they believe they are right. I have learned not to ignore and swap my truths in favour of somebody else's, for fear of being wrong or being rejected, and instead am learning to stand in my own strength.

Disagreements are often simply projections of our inner worlds onto another, while showing our pain. I learned that if somebody gives you the gift of anger, sadness, disappointment, or expectation, then if you don't accept their gift by reacting to it, they must keep it and hold on to it. In turn they must look at their own emotional projections and most of the time people don't like that.

I had grown so much in my time away. I had transformed in a way I could never have imagined, with an abundance of learning experience which I could never have attained if I had stayed at home.

My experience with Tom had propelled me into a journey of self-enquiry, forcing me to listen to my body and hear the inner voice within. It had shown me that I had ignored the little girl inside who simply wanted to be seen, who wanted to be told she was safe, loved and that her truth mattered. It mattered to me. Ayahuasca had taught me to be kind to myself; it had taught me patience and calm.

My travels had been a means of survival. I needed to get away and find myself. It was all chance and yet it all seemed like a

Divine plan. Everything happens for a reason, and I truly feel that when we are in flow with the Universe, she delivers the most beautiful synchronicities when we are awake and ready to receive them with open arms.

Upon returning home I discovered that growth comes from sharing your world and experiences with others. While traveling, learning, studying, and gathering the wisdom and knowledge in every country I visited; while doing all that work on myself, and uncovering who I truly was, I could have never known what it was leading to. I was simply following my flow. I was simply surrendering to the Universe and going where I needed to, when I needed to. When I came home from traveling it took some time to figure out, it took a few years of fumbling and making mistakes, but I eventually realised what my role was here. It took some time to make a real start (and believe me there is a whole book in that journey alone). My old job was waiting for me, but I found it difficult to settle back into the 9 to 5 world, so I undertook lots more training courses in the modalities I had learned on my travels; and then I started my own business.

As an Holistic Therapist, I now show women how to survive, thrive and shine in their life. I use a combination of practical tools and intuitive guidance as well as Reiki, Reflexology, Astrology, Life Path Coaching and so much more, to help people come home to themselves. The wisdom I was gathering and tools I was learning, would all become part of the Soul Survival toolkit I now share with my clients. I now teach my 'Intrepid Soul Navigation' System, both as a one to one and group coach, mentor, and therapist. Something I could never have imagined would come from all the mayhem where I initially felt life had ended. Had I not been through everything you have read in these three books; I would never have found my calling. In many ways, all of what happened served to wake me up from my slumber. My mess became my message. To help others, I first needed to help myself. I needed to know I was lost, I needed to search for myself and needed to know what it meant to find myself, also.

My Intrepid Soul Navigation system now helps other women, do the same. I feel it is as important to understand our human journey as is it our spiritual journey, integrating the knowledge and wisdom that comes from both. Our bodies hold the key to our spiritual enlightenment in this world, and there is so much we have yet to learn, if we just knew how to listen more. Perhaps this whole human experience is about finding ourselves and in turn finding our way back home, through the perfect imperfection of it all; it may not always be smooth but there are always opportunities for growth. Life is short; I had seen that with my Dad, and unpredictably, I had seen that with Tom. However, it was also for living and I was about to begin a new adventure with Piers. He had given up his life in the UK to be with me in Ireland, to merge with my family, to love me for who I was and to fully embrace the journey ahead. We finally moved in together, no more saying Goodbye at airports or meeting up in other countries, no more texting and phone calls or emails and videos long distance. For so long we had craved to be together, to hold each other and never let go, to look into each other's eyes and feel that one-ness. Now we would get to wake up every day together, we got to kiss each other goodnight as we fell asleep with the warmth of our bodies together. I had missed that closeness while away travelling; something which became so much clearer to me. Being in the energetic presence of somebody we love, is so important.

And what lay ahead, neither of us knew at the time. But we both knew it hadn't been co-incidence we had met. We knew our hearts would always be as one. But hearts as one, doesn't always mean as one together. Was it too much to hope that Fairy tales could be real? I knew Disney had a lot to answer for and in

Pop Culture, the 'Twin Flame' dynamic is certainly something which had been romanticised and popularised in our culture; it became something I would question over time. Would it be too much to wish for a happy ending, after all we had been through together - or was that a delusion of grandeur? The struggles we had at the beginning were now starting to show some cracks. I was unsure where it would all go, but I knew for certain only time would tell....

***

ACKNOWLEDEGMENTS

My heartfelt thanks to all the beautiful Souls who have walked with me on this crazy but magical journey we call life. To all those who have welcomed me into their hearts just as I am. To all those who have supported me in my stepping into a more authentic and intuitive version of myself. To all those who took a chance on me, believed in me, and were there for me when I needed you the most – I am forever in gratitude.

To my Mother: in more ways than one, I would not be here had it not been for you. You have quite literally allowed me to open and bloom like a flower. You have been the light and beacon in every storm. For you I will never have enough words, or books of words, to convey my never-ending love, appreciation, depth of gratitude, and bond with you. 'I don't know if you know, but when we miss each other so, Look up... I'll meet you at the moon' (Imelda May) XXX

To my Father: Thank you for being You! For showing me what it means to be a Healer, a daughter, and a friend. You always believed in me, listened to me, and saw the strength and will in me before I ever knew it myself. You always encouraged me to follow my heart, not to worry about what others think and you taught me so much of the healing gifts I have today. Whenever my heart broke or I lost myself, you were always there for me; allowing me to make mistakes and encouraging me to be my person in the world. Even after death, your guiding hand helped me turn some of the most challenging moments of my life into gold. I miss you so much and I Love you XXXX.

To my Brothers: Thank you both for your love, support and always listening to me saying 'Do you remember when we were kids …' As an incredibly nostalgic creature, I can say I had such a wonderful childhood with you both. I often miss the simple days. No words can express how much I love you both. Thank you for your imprints XX.

To Anna: with your kindness, compassion, wisdom, and generosity you opened the door and gave me the opportunities to heal myself in ways I could never have imagined possible. Your healing gifts and incredible depth of heart offered me the strength and support to embrace my own healing talents. Your belief in me and encouragement to step into my power, when I was unable to do it for myself, I can never have enough words to thank you with.

For YOU, I am truly grateful XX.

To Damien: my beautiful friend. Your strength, support, courage, wisdom, and boundless tenacity have influenced so much of both who I am as a person, and as an entrepreneur. Though you are no longer with us, I can often feel your energy. I know you are looking over my shoulder, giving me the strength to believe in myself, like you have always done. You saw in me what I could not see in myself, and you have been such an integral part of my journey. You were the rock and life raft in some of my darkest moments. I miss you terribly XX.

To my Dearest Friend Erica: I feel truly blessed to have you in my life. I always feel the fullest expression of who I am is nurtured, supported, and in bloom, in your presence. Although we are oceans apart, I feel constantly inspired by your love. You are a truly beautiful soul as a Mother, a wife, an entrepreneur, a Healer, a creative, and most of all, a friend.

Thank you to Lizzy Shortall who I began this journey, as a writing buddy. Having accountability for each other as we birthed our first books together, was a beautiful experience.

Thank you also to my Beta Readers who gave such amazing feedback on my books. I am glad it was a rollercoaster you enjoyed. To those who gave me huge confidence in knowing I was doing the right thing by releasing this into the world. I am so grateful my words have already begun to help so many, even before it was published. Thank you, Maryam Nawaz, on Fiverr from Pakistan, who was an incredible help in formatting my books and taking the stress out of getting my books up and online. To Lisa Jane of Butterfly Creation, for helping me format my book covers to get them online. To Carrie Green, the FEA, and all my friends and connections in the Online Business world, as well as my Astrology, Reiki, and Herbal friends; all of who have been an incredible source of support through this process.

Thank you to all my Teachers, Mentors, the Elders of our communities, my Ancestors whose torch I bear and whose wisdom I endeavour to pass on as best I can, while walking this road. Thank you to my Guides, and those who are both seen and unseen, who are forever in my heart. What an opportunity to be born in these times.

***

ABOUT THE AUTHOR

Deborah J. Kelly was born a country girl in the rural South East of Ireland. She now lives in the suburbs of Dublin. She is a Holistic Therapist, Speaker, Reiki Teacher, Astrologist, Mentor, Podcast Creator, Artist, Entrepreneur, and Writer.

As a child, she was creative, quiet, and a curious wee thing. She loved spending time in nature whether watching activities in the grass beneath her feet, playing in the trees, splashing in ponds, picking blackberries, making mud pies, or watching the stars above in the night sky. Fascinated by nature and the human experience, even as a small girl, she would ask herself 'What is it all about?'

She loved to write poetry and journal. She enjoyed writing short stories and creating cartoons and comics. She loved to record and play DJ on her radio, something she would later turn her skills to as a Podcast host and creator of 'The Intrepid Wisdom Podcast' (www.intrepidwisdom.com available on Spotify & iTunes). Deborah also loved to sketch and draw. She was always participating in whatever local art competitions were available. Nicknamed by her primary school teacher as 'The Doodler' she had more art supplies and sketch pads than an art and hobby shop. Upon leaving school she attended NCAD (National College of Art & Design). She worked full time as a Care Assistant to people with severe disabilities. She later returned to studying, specialising in Interior Design and Interior Architecture. After this, she worked in small start-up and medium-sized furniture and design companies. Here she worked in sales, design, admin, office manager, marketing and advertising, accounts, etc. Due to her experience in these businesses, she learned the ins and outs of entrepreneurism and of running a company. This was something that she would later apply while setting up her own Holistic business.

Through the years Deborah has travelled around the world and studied many subjects at home and abroad, from Hypnotherapy/ Psychotherapy to Reiki, Reflexology, Astrology, Meditation, Herbal Medicine, Mayan Cosmology, Acupressure and so much more. She has, and still, collects wisdom from around the world as a means of sharing these practical tools with others.

Little would she know it at the time, but she was always on a quest for truth, wisdom, and understanding. This would be an integral part of her journey and life's work. Understanding the Human Experience, Eldership, the role, and importance of practical, natural healing and Wisdom, is a huge passion for Deborah. Through this she has created the unique 'Intrepid Soul Navigation System' which brings all the modalities she has studied, through the years and across the globe, together to help others uncover their true self, to reconnect with their inner wisdom and learn how to interpret their world, so they too can navigate life with ease.

As a Holistic Therapist and Speaker practicing and sharing her wisdom and knowledge around the world; she is based in Dublin and has clients in Ireland, the UK, Canada, the USA, Australia, and further afield. She has her own private practice where she sees clients in person and online.

You can contact Deborah J. Kelly and request her as a Guest Speaker, contact her for Guest Podcasting or Interviews, and you can work with her directly, by emailing her at deborahjsoulnavigation@gmail.com or check out her website www.deborahjkelly.com. You will also find her on Social Media as Deborah J. Kelly Intrepid Soul Navigation.

***

Printed in Great Britain
by Amazon